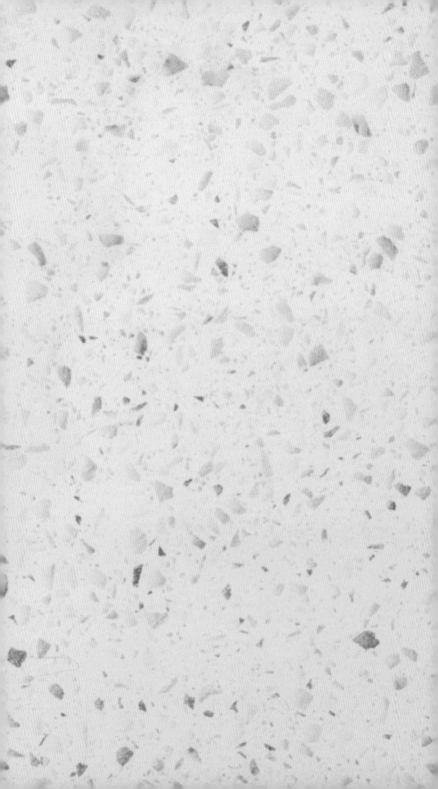

Sauce Up Your Boards

Boards

MORE THAN 250 RECIPES FOR CONDIMENTS, DIPS, JAMS & SPREADS

HILLARY DAVIS

Photographs by Sheena Bates

Gibbs Smith

First Edition

28 27 26 25 24   5 4 3 2 1

Text © 2024 Hillary Davis
Photographs © 2024 Sheena Bates

Published by
Gibbs Smith
570 N. Sportsplex Drive
Kaysville, UT 84037

1.800.835.4993 orders
www.gibbs-smith.com

Designed by Ryan Thomann
Production design by Renee Bond
Printed and bound in China

Library of Congress Control Number: 2023952559
ISBN: 978-1-4236-6724-7

This product is made of FSC®-certified and other controlled material.

FSC®
www.fsc.org

MIX
Paper | Supporting
responsible forestry
FSC® C153458

Contents

Introduction

AS I GREW UP, there was always a lazy Susan on the kitchen and dining room tables that carried our favorite honeys, jams, bottles of Tabasco and Worcestershire, salts, and mustards. For dinner, my father would often add small bowls of sauces or dips to enjoy. When we sat down for a meal, my brother and I would peek over to see what new offerings were there and talk about which one we liked better or not at all.

I didn't know they were called condiments. I just knew it was fun to have a choice of things to sprinkle, spoon, or pour.

My love for that experience increased exponentially one summer when I was a teenager visiting a friend whose mother made beef fondue one night and offered a sampling of six different sauces arranged down the center of the table that we could dip our pieces of just-cooked beef into. Dinner became a party and the sauces were so enjoyable that it eased our teenage angst at being seated with newly made friends at a formal dining table. Sauces broke the ice. *Who knew?* And it brought us all together in a fun way.

I took those memories into my own home as a newlywed. If I had a burger night for friends, I would set up a "burger bar" with all sorts of condiments and toppings next to the tray of burgers and buns. On spaghetti night, I would present the pasta in a big bowl on the kitchen counter and next to it a variety of three or four sauces, grated cheese, hot pepper flakes, and a mountain of fresh basil leaves.

And then we moved to France, and I discovered a nation of condiment lovers. I felt right at home.

Supermarkets I visited had what seemed like endlessly long rows of jams, whole rows of just mustards, vinegars and oils as far as you could see, and dozens of artisan butters. And they were flavored. And fun.

I soon discovered beautiful hand-wrought olive wood boards for sale in village shops. Some were long and made to hold baguettes. Some were wider to hold a fleet of cheeses. Some were used to gather jams and butter. Now, instead of a lazy Susan like the one on my family's table, I used these hand-carved, golden-brown boards to display my condiments.

So if I served gazpacho, for example, whether for friends or for just the two of us, I would arrange several toppings on a beautiful long olive wood board, small bowls of chopped red, yellow, and green peppers, chopped onion, chopped cucumber, croutons, and sometimes shrimp. Almost every night I put out a board with ramekins of homemade butter and a couple of flavored savory butters to enjoy on a warm baguette.

When I would serve curry, I would put out little bowls lined up on a board with grated coconut, chopped peanuts, lime pickle, chutneys, mint sauce, and more. Even when I served dessert, I placed a long narrow tray down the center of the table with a line of toppings and treats. When I served brisket or a roast, I offered a board with homemade mustards and salts and a horseradish sauce.

I learned a long time ago that the surprise and interest people feel when they first approach a meal you have made, offering them choices of flavorings to add, always sparks conversation and participation. I like that it brings people together in a communal experience around my table.

People linger around a board.

I'll have guests walk into the kitchen for a luncheon spread and hear them say, "Oh look! She has different kinds of chili crunch oil to try! Look, there's Momofuku, Trader Joe's . . . so cool." That brings others to come and see and conversation is sparked. It brings people together.

And I like that there is creativity on my side in pulling it together for them. Sometimes I make one board with homemade condiments, and next to it offer another board of store-bought favorites for a tasting comparison.

In my house, it's all about condiments.

I can't tell you how many store-bought condiments are typically found in my pantry and refrigerator! I am a condiment junkie and I admit it.

Equally, I am wild about making my own. One, because it is something I love to tinker with, but two because most store-bought condiments are old, have expiration dates months in the future, and may be made with preservatives, additives, MSG, corn syrup, and artificial flavors and dyes. You've just made a healthy clean meal then drizzle on condiments full of chemicals, artificial flavors, dyes, palm oil, gums, and more? So when I use store-bought, I try to buy healthier alternatives. Or make my own.

Making your own takes mere minutes and you can enjoy fresh vibrant condiments that are good for you—with no chemicals added.

Additive free. Clean. Fresh. Absolutely delicious!

So join me in making superstar, small-batch, homemade mustards, fresh herbal salts, ketchup, dips, and savory and sweet sauces to share down the center of your table to *sauce up your boards*! The following recipes and ideas will provide you with everything you need to know to create beautiful condiments for any occasion.

What is a condiment?

A pinch of this. A few drizzles of that. A ladle of sauce.

To me, it's the best part of the meal. A tantalizing flavor bomb that takes a dish to a memorable level.

Condiments add flavor. What would shrimp cocktail be without a knock-out cocktail sauce to dip it into? Spring rolls on their own? No. They need to be twirled into the most amazing pool of sauce. Salad without dressing? Caesar salad would fall flat without its garlicky-anchovy blanket of goodness. And don't get me started on sweets. I revel in mouthwatering hot fudge sauce or hot salted caramel sauce draped over cold vanilla ice cream. Bang. I flick a few flakes of smoked crunchy sea salt on top. *Awesome.*

And that, my dear friends and cooks, is what a condiment is. It lets you cook with flair and with the freedom to add wonderful, delicious layers of flavor, perhaps from a mix of cultures, to your own down-home cooking. Whether from traveling or from memories of our grandmothers who came from Mexico or France or Portugal or Taiwan, we have come in contact with flavors from other countries that we all like to weave into our recipes.

For instance, tonight I am making a big bowl of angel-hair pasta for some friends. I have four lovely sauces I want to offer them in separate bowls in the middle of the table on a condiment board. One is from Italy, a basil pesto made in the Piedmont region that uses walnuts instead of pine nuts. Another is a sauce that I learned from my next-door neighbor in France made with white wine and fresh clams. Another is a Greek feta and shrimp sauce, and the fourth is one of my favorites, a pad thai–inspired peanut and cilantro sauce, because, why not? The sauces are condiments, and they will make the meal special and delicious.

My philosophy in cooking is to use incomparably fresh, and hopefully organic, produce to make a lovingly prepared meal. Then I dress it up with condiments to go to the party.

Because a pizza is no longer mundane when it is drizzled with hot honey. Brunch lights up when a selection of homemade jams and butters are presented on a tasting board. A bagel-and-lox board is transformed with a fleet of little pots of homemade cream cheese blended with berries or salmon. Simple food can be made glamorous with the exotic, colorful, exciting additions of condiments.

What is a condiment board?

It is a tasting board. Much like charcuterie boards, condiment boards gather together in one place a variety of offerings for people to enjoy and share. It can be set in the middle of a table, on a counter, even on a picnic blanket, and holds tasty embellishments for the food at hand.

For example, when I serve brunch to family or friends, I put out a couple of long boards, platters, or narrow trays. One will hold colorful jams, all in a row with spoons before each one. Another will hold my homemade butters: cinnamon roll butter, fresh smashed strawberry butter, and wild-flower honey butter with big crunchy flakes of sea salt on top.

For all meals, I usually have a board—long, round, square or of wood, silver, copper or glass—offering a selection of salts in salt cellars and pepper grinders with white, black, or mixed-color peppercorns.

You get the idea! And there are no rules. That's where the creativity comes in. Whatever you can imagine, or want to try making, you can put on your board. Your family and friends will enjoy it, because condiments can change an average meal into a great one. A variety of condiments is even better. To present your condiments, have fun with different kinds of receptacles.

HERE ARE SOME IDEAS TO GET YOU STARTED

BOARDS: Any shape will work—square, rectangle, long, or oblong. Wood, metal, stone, sterling silver trays, even a mirror would be fabulous!

BOTTLES: I use Kilner glass bottles with stoppers for vinegars and oils, or empty wine bottles with stoppers.

BOWLS: I keep a variety such as small 4-inch bowls, 6- to 8-ounce rame-kins, copper bowls, cut glass bowls, butter warmers, three or four square white shallow bowls to line up on a board, flea market mismatched bowls and small saucers, and mini cast-iron skillets.

DIPPING OIL DISHES: These can be small shallow bowls, round Asian-style shallow sauce dishes, butter warmers, and even ramekins.

EQUIPMENT: An immersion blender, mortar and pestle, spice grinder, coffee grinder, food processor, mini food processor, and blender are all helpful for preparing items for a board.

JARS: I frequently use short and medium Ball canning jars and short and tall Weck jars.

LABELS: To truly enjoy the variety of the condiments on your boards, rather than leaving them anonymous, label each one. You can use chalkboards as your board to hold them and chalk on their names; or use sticky printer labels for jars and bottles, even colored Post-it Notes identifying each condiment along a wooden board will do!

SALT CELLARS: Bamboo, crystal, marble, stainless steel, modern Italian-design ones, even colorful handmade pottery salt cellars found online and in home shops are perfect little serving devices.

SERVING PIECES: Think small: small forks, small spoons, small tongs, tooth-picks, 1-ounce stainless steel ladles, Asian-style white porcelain soup spoons, tasting spoons, salt spoons, honey spool, mini cast-iron skillets, ramekins, mini bowls, and mini milk pitchers.

Condiment ideas for your pantry

You should see my pantry. Shelves and shelves of condiments, stacked and orderly. Some have labels in another language from halfway across the world and some are from a farm shop down the road a bit.

My pantry is my insurance policy that I can whip up something delicious to eat, relying almost totally on what I can find there, and in my refrigerator, where I store many of my store-bought add-ons and homemade specialties.

This is what I normally keep on hand, the brands and flavors I am loyal to.

MY STORE-BOUGHT PANTRY STAPLES

CHOCOLATE

Bar of good white chocolate
Bar of Valrhona dark
    bittersweet chocolate
Chocolate chips

DRIED SPICES AND HERBS

Allspice, ground
Basil
Bay leaves
Cayenne pepper
Celery salt
Chinese five-spice powder
Chives
Cinnamon, ground and whole
Cloves, ground and whole
Cumin, ground
Curry powder
Dill
Garlic powder
Ginger, ground
Herbes de Provence
Juniper berries
Knorr Aromat Seasoning
Knorr beef, chicken, and
    vegetable bouillon cubes
McCormick pickling spice
Mustard seed, yellow and brown,
    dry mustard powder
Nutmeg, ground and whole
Old Bay Seasoning
Onion powder
Oregano
Paprika, smoked Spanish, sweet
    Hungarian, *piment d'Espelette*
Parsley
Peppercorns, whole red,
    green, and black
Red pepper flakes
Rosemary
Sage
Star anise, whole
Tarragon
Thyme
Turmeric

FREEZER CONDIMENTS

Frozen berries and fruits
Ice cream
Sorbets

JAMS

Bitter orange marmalade
Bonne Maman jams
Chivers Lemon Curd
Fig jam
Hero Apricot Jam
Tiptree Ginger jam
Tiptree Little Scarlet Strawberry jam

KETCHUP

Primal Kitchen Organic Ketchup
Sir Kensington Ketchup
Trader Joe's Ketchup

MAYONNAISE

Hellmann's Mayonnaise
Kewpie Japanese Mayonnaise
Sir Kensington Organic Mayonnaise.

MUSTARD

French Amora mustard
Pommery Moutarde de Meaux
Pommery Moutarde de Meaux
    Royale with Cognac

NUTS

Almonds
Hazelnuts
Pistachios
Walnuts

OILS

Avocado oil, high-quality
Chili crunch oil
Nicolas Alziari French olive oil
Opio French olive oil
Toasted sesame oil.
Villa Cappelli Puglian Italian olive oil

SALTS

A.Vogel Herbamare Sea Salt
Baleine fine sea salt
Celtic fine sea salt
Himalayan pink salt
Maldon Regular Sea Salt Flakes
Maldon Smoked Sea Salt Flakes

STORE-BOUGHT REFRIGERATOR CONDIMENTS

Cheeses
Crème fraîche
Fermented sauerkraut
Good French butters
Heavy whipping cream
Kimchi
Miso, sweet white
Prepared horseradish
Sour cream
Yogurt, plain Greek

SWEETENERS

Brown sugar, dark and light brown
Confectioners' sugar
Granulated sugar
Honey
Molasses
Muscovado sugar
Sanding sugar

VINEGARS

Bragg Apple Cider Vinegar
Champagne vinegar
Chinese black vinegar
Colavita White Balsamic Vinegar
Dark balsamic vinegar
Distilled white vinegar
Marukan Rice Wine Vinegar
Pommery Sherry Vinegar
Red wine vinegar
Tarragon vinegar

OTHER

Anchovies, paste in a tube,
    flat fillets in a tin
Capers
Cocoa powder, unsweetened
Cornichons
Dessert wines and liquors
Dulce de leche, canned

Hoisin sauce
Instant espresso powder
Italian Amarena cherries
Kalamata pitted olives
Korean Gochujang
Marinated artichoke hearts, jarred
Marinated mushrooms, jarred
Mirin
Olives
Panko breadcrumbs
Pickles
Ponzu
Preserved lemons, jarred
Relishes
Soy sauce
Sriracha
Tabasco and Frank's Red Hot sauces
Tapenade, jarred
Thai sweet chili sauce
Worcestershire sauce

Mayonnaise

I GREW UP THINKING mayonnaise should be slathered on everything. My father literally swiped it on his toast before topping it with a poached egg in the morning. He swirled it into our scrambled eggs, used gobs of it on our lunch sandwiches, thickly layered it on fish before baking or grilling, and loved it as a snack on almost anything munchable. So naturally I keep it on hand and quickly whip up my own when in the mood. In my house, we use it on a daily basis.

Homemade has a different flavor profile than store-bought mayonnaise and it's a treat you will grow to love. Here are some basic recipes along with some variations for you to try. I will often make two or three of these for a condiment board, then add one or two store-bought ones to it as well. The best method I have found to make mayonnaise is in a blender or with a stick immersion blender in a Mason jar. The immersion blender method is the easiest and fastest and I provide a recipe for it below as well as the blender recipe.

Use fresh, free-range eggs for the best result.

As for oils when making mayonnaise, using all olive oil will produce a stronger taste which marries well with tuna, shrimp, or tapas. Using an oil like avocado oil will produce a more neutral-tasting mayonnaise which can then take on the characteristics of flavorings you add to it.

I like to use half neutral oil and half olive oil when I make my mayonnaise. And I sometimes use rice wine vinegar instead of lemon juice to give my mayonnaise a slightly sweet taste. You can use tarragon vinegar, red wine vinegar, lemon or lime juice, or any kind of acid you like. If you have any leftover homemade mayonnaise, be sure to store it in the refrigerator for up to five days.

Basic Blender Mayonnaise

MAKES ABOUT 1¼ CUPS

1 large egg, room temperature
1 large egg yolk, room temperature
2 teaspoons Dijon mustard
½ cup avocado oil (or any
   other neutral oil)

½ cup olive oil
¼ teaspoon fine sea salt,
   or more to taste
3 teaspoons freshly
   squeezed lemon juice

In the blender, process the egg and egg yolk for 30 seconds. Drop by drop, start adding the oil, pausing between drops, for the first 40 seconds. Then add a very thin stream of oil while processing, pausing once in a while. Have patience and keep adding in a very thin stream. It could take a couple of minutes to come together. Only then, when the mixture has reached the consistency of mayonnaise, do you add the salt and lemon juice and beat to combine.

Basic Immersion Stick Mayonnaise

MAKES ABOUT 1¼ CUPS

1 large egg, room temperature
1 teaspoon Dijon mustard
½ cup avocado oil (or any
   other neutral oil)
½ cup olive oil

¼ teaspoon fine sea salt,
   or more to taste
3 teaspoons freshly
   squeezed lemon juice

Toss all the ingredients into a Mason jar or tall cylindrical container. Using an immersion stick blender, pulse until the mixture attains a mayonnaise consistency. It should only take a minute.

Aïoli Mayonnaise

MAKES 1 CUP

1 cup mayonnaise of choice
3 garlic cloves, sliced, or
  more if needed
¼ teaspoon fine sea salt

Combine all the ingredients
into a blender and process
until smooth. Add more garlic if
you prefer and blend again.

Hot Honey Chili Crisp Mayonnaise

MAKES ½ CUP

½ cup mayonnaise of choice
2 tablespoons hot honey
1½ teaspoons chili crisp/
  crunch oil, crisp bits only

Whisk all the ingredients
together in a bowl.

Honey Mustard Mayonnaise

MAKES ¾ CUP

½ cup mayonnaise of choice
2 tablespoons honey
¼ cup Dijon mustard
1 teaspoon apple cider vinegar
⅛ teaspoon fine sea salt

Whisk together all the
ingredients in a bowl.

Sweet Curried Mayonnaise

MAKES ABOUT 1¼ CUPS

1 cup mayonnaise of choice
4 teaspoons curry powder
3 tablespoons apricot jam
Raisins, to taste (optional)
1 tablespoon coconut
    flakes (optional)

Combine the mayonnaise, curry powder, and apricot jam in a blender or food processor and process until smooth. At this point I often fold in raisins and/or coconut flakes, but this is purely optional.

Danish Rémoulade

MAKES 1½ CUPS

½ cup sweet relish
1 thick slice Granny Smith apple,
    grated on a box grater
2 teaspoons minced or
    grated red onion

1 cup mayonnaise of choice
1 teaspoon granulated sugar
3 teaspoons yellow mustard powder
¼ teaspoon ground turmeric

Layer 2 or 3 paper towels, place the relish on top, and enclose the relish inside. Squeeze, over the sink, until any liquid is drained. Transfer the relish to a bowl. Add the rest of the ingredients and whisk to combine.

Chipotle Mayonnaise

MAKES ABOUT 1¼ CUPS

1 cup mayonnaise of choice
2 chipotle peppers (in adobo
    sauce from a can)
1 tablespoon plus 1 teaspoon
    adobo sauce from the can

1 teaspoon freshly squeezed
    lemon juice
1 teaspoon honey
1 teaspoon ketchup

Combine all the ingredients in a blender or food processor and process until smooth.

Wasabi Mayonnaise

MAKES ½ CUP

2 tablespoons wasabi paste
⅛ teaspoon fine sea salt
½ cup mayonnaise of choice
1 teaspoon garlic powder
1 teaspoon soy sauce

Combine all the ingredients in a bowl and whisk until well blended.

Kimchi Aïoli

MAKES ABOUT 1¼ CUPS

1 cup mayonnaise of choice
¼ cup finely chopped
    Classic Red Kimchi
1 garlic clove, minced, or
    more if needed
1 teaspoon juice from kimchi jar

1 teaspoon seasoned rice vinegar
1 teaspoon sesame oil

Combine all the ingredients in a bowl and mix until well blended.

Green Herby Mayonnaise

MAKES 1½ CUPS

¼ cup tightly packed
   fresh basil leaves
¼ cup fresh Italian flat-
   leaf parsley leaves
¼ cup fresh dill fronds
2 garlic cloves, sliced
1 teaspoon Dijon mustard

1 tablespoon freshly
   squeezed lemon juice
¼ teaspoon fine sea salt
½ teaspoon granulated sugar
⅛ teaspoon cayenne pepper
1 ¼ cups mayonnaise of choice
Extra-virgin olive oil, if needed

Combine all the ingredients, except for the mayonnaise, in a blender or food processor and pulse until the herbs are finely minced. Transfer the mixture to a bowl, add the mayonnaise, and whisk to blend. Taste for seasoning and add more salt if desired. If you would like it thinner, add a tiny splash of water or a bit of oil and whisk again.

Pesto Mayonnaise

MAKES 1½ CUPS

1 cup basil leaves, tightly packed
2 garlic cloves, sliced
¼ teaspoon fine sea salt
2 tablespoons freshly
   squeezed lemon juice
1 cup mayonnaise of choice

¼ cup grated or shredded
   Parmesan cheese
Extra-virgin olive oil, if needed

Combine the basil leaves, garlic, and salt in a food processor and process until finely minced. Add the lemon juice, mayonnaise, and cheese and process until well blended. Thin with a bit of olive oil if desired.

Citrusy Ponzu Mayonnaise

MAKES 1 CUP

1 cup mayonnaise of choice
2 teaspoons ponzu (citrus-
   flavored soy sauce)

Blend the ingredients in a
bowl with a whisk or fork.

Cacio e Pepe Mayonnaise

MAKES ABOUT 1½ CUPS

1 tablespoon whole black
   peppercorns
1 cup mayonnaise of choice

½ cup freshly grated
   Parmesan cheese
¼ teaspoon fine sea salt

Put the peppercorns in a small plastic bag and crush them with a rolling pin
until they almost look white (alternatively, pulse or coarsely grind them in
a coffee grinder or spice mill). Transfer the crushed peppercorns to a bowl,
add the rest of the ingredients, and whisk to combine.

Blue Cheese Mayonnaise

MAKES ABOUT 1¼ CUPS

1 cup mayonnaise of choice
4 ounces crumbled blue cheese,
   room temperature
2 garlic cloves, sliced

⅛ teaspoon fine sea salt,
   or more if needed
¼ teaspoon hot sauce,
   or more if needed

Combine all the ingredients in a blender and process until smooth. Taste and
add more salt and/or hot sauce, if desired.

Ketchup

IF YOU LOOK AT any online survey of the most popular condiment around the world, ketchup is usually at the top of the list or very near it. It is a condiment beloved by children and anyone who loves French fries!

Yet most commercial brands list high-fructose corn syrup as one of the main ingredients, as well as chemical preservatives, which may or may not be what you want you or your children to consume in great quantities.

So the first two recipes in this chapter offer you the chance to make your own ketchup in order to control the ingredients that go into it. For the recipes that follow, you can choose to use either your homemade version or store-bought.

If I were serving a burger bar, I would definitely make a couple of homemade ketchups to add to a condiment board, especially surprising ones that people wouldn't expect to see, like my Tangy and Sweet Blueberry Ketchup (page 26). I once had a version in a trendy pub on a burger and came right home to play with ingredients. I love the way it turned out. It goes so well with ham or burgers. Then I would also offer a couple of good store-bought ones that everyone loves and expects to see!

Quick Basic Ketchup

MAKES 2 CUPS

2 (6-ounce) cans tomato paste
2 tablespoons water
4 tablespoons apple cider vinegar
    or white balsamic vinegar
1 teaspoon olive oil
5 tablespoons dark brown sugar
    or half sugar and half honey

¼ teaspoon fine sea salt
½ teaspoon onion powder
⅛ teaspoon garlic powder
⅛ teaspoon ground allspice
½ teaspoon ground cinnamon
¼ teaspoon ground cloves

Combine all the ingredients in a saucepan and whisk them together. Warm over medium heat while whisking, for about 3 minutes or until the sugars dissolve. Take the pan off the heat and transfer the mixture to glass jar(s) with a screw top. Allow to cool to room temperature, screw on the lids, and store in the refrigerator for up to 1 month.

Guava Ketchup

MAKES 4 CUPS

2 cups ketchup of choice
2 cups guava paste, sliced or a
    (17-ounce) jar guava jelly

2 tablespoons water
½ teaspoon ground allspice

Combine all the ingredients in a saucepan and bring to a boil. Lower the heat to medium and stir until the guava paste has dissolved. Add a splash more water if desired. Transfer to glass jar(s) with a screw top and allow to cool to room temperature. Screw on the lids and store in the refrigerator for up to 1 month. The ketchup tends to thicken in the refrigerator so bring it to room temperature before serving or whisk in 1 tablespoon of water before serving.

Fresh Tomato Ketchup

MAKES 2 CUPS

2 pounds ripe Roma tomatoes,
  coarsely chopped
½ cup distilled white vinegar
3 tablespoons extra-virgin olive oil
½ teaspoon fine sea salt
6 tablespoons light brown sugar
3 large garlic cloves, sliced
1 red Fresno or green jalapeño
  pepper, sliced, seeded

1 Vidalia or yellow onion,
  coarsely chopped
2 bay leaves
1 cinnamon stick
½ teaspoon celery seeds
1 teaspoon ground cinnamon
1 teaspoon ground cloves
½ teaspoon ground allspice

Combine all the ingredients in a large pot or Dutch oven and cook over medium heat for 30 to 40 minutes, or until everything is soft. Remove the bay leaves and cinnamon stick and discard.

Pour the mixture into a blender and process until smooth, or use an immersion blender to blend.

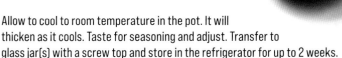

Transfer the mixture back to the pot and cook over medium heat until thickened to a ketchup consistency, about 30 minutes.

Allow to cool to room temperature in the pot. It will thicken as it cools. Taste for seasoning and adjust. Transfer to glass jar(s) with a screw top and store in the refrigerator for up to 2 weeks.

Spicy Sriracha Ketchup

MAKES 1 CUP

1 cup ketchup of choice
4 tablespoons sriracha
1 tablespoon light brown sugar

Whisk everything together in a bowl and serve. Transfer to glass jar(s) with a screw top and store in the refrigerator.

Tangy and Sweet Blueberry Ketchup

MAKES 2 CUPS

2 tablespoons extra-virgin olive oil
1 medium shallot, finely chopped
3 large garlic cloves, minced
3 tablespoons tomato paste
½ cup dark brown sugar
4 cups fresh or frozen
    blueberries, divided

¼ cup apple cider vinegar
½ teaspoon fine sea salt
⅛ teaspoon ground cloves
¼ teaspoon ground cinnamon
1 teaspoon Dijon mustard

Heat a saucepan over medium heat. Add the oil, shallot, and garlic and cook for 5 minutes, or until the shallot has softened. Add the tomato paste, brown sugar, 3 cups of blueberries, vinegar, salt, cloves, and cinnamon, stir well, and bring to a boil. Lower the heat to maintain a low rolling boil and cook for 12 to 15 minutes, or until slightly thickened.

Allow the mixture to cool to room temperature. Transfer to a blender or food processor and process until very smooth. Taste for seasoning and adjust. Coarsely chop the remaining 1 cup of blueberries and stir them into the ketchup. Serve or transfer to glass jar(s) with a screw top and store in the refrigerator for up to 2 weeks.

Rhubarb Ketchup

MAKES 2 CUPS

2 cups 1-inch pieces fresh rhubarb
1 medium red onion, finely chopped
1 medium shallot, finely chopped
1 cup canned diced
    tomatoes, drained
2 large garlic cloves, sliced
¼ cup apple cider vinegar

2 or 3 tablespoons
    tomato paste, to taste
3 tablespoons dark brown
    sugar, or more if needed
½ teaspoon ground cloves
½ teaspoon ground cumin
1 teaspoon ground cinnamon
¼ teaspoon fine sea salt

Combine all the ingredients in a large saucepan and cook, stirring often, over medium heat for about 30 minutes, or until thickened.

Cool to room temperature. At this point, you can purée it a blender to make a smooth ketchup or leave as is. Transfer to glass jar(s) with a screw top and store in the refrigerator for up to 1 week.

Filipino-Style Banana Ketchup

MAKES 1½ CUPS

3 large garlic cloves, sliced
½ cup tightly packed finely chopped red onion
1 medium jalapeño pepper, stemmed, sliced, keep seeds
1 (2-inch) piece ginger, peeled, thinly sliced
½ cup neutral oil
2 tablespoons tomato paste

1 teaspoon ground allspice
⅛ teaspoon ground cloves
1 teaspoon ground cinnamon
4 really ripe bananas, with brown spots on the skin, sliced
¼ cup rice vinegar or white balsamic
½ teaspoon Tabasco sauce
¾ cup light brown sugar
¼ tablespoon fine sea salt

Combine the garlic, onion, jalapeño, ginger, and oil in a food processor and process until well combined, then pour the mixture into a large saucepan. Cook over medium heat, stirring frequently, until the liquid reduces and the oil in the bottom of the saucepan is bubbling. Add the tomato paste and cook for 3 minutes, or until it's combined and the oil has taken on the color of the tomato paste. Add the allspice, cloves, and cinnamon and stir for 1 minute.

In the same food processor, combine the bananas, vinegar, and Tabasco and process until smooth. Add a little water if needed to process. Pour the banana mixture into the saucepan and whisk to combine. Add the brown sugar and simmer, stirring often, for 10 to 15 minutes or until thickened. Add the salt and whisk. Taste and add more vinegar, sugar, or salt to your taste.

Transfer to glass jar(s) with a screw top and allow to cool to room temperature. Screw on the lids and store in the refrigerator for up to 5 days.

Mustard

IF THERE IS ONE condiment I can't live without, it is mustard. James Beard wrote an article for *Esquire Magazine* in 1975 titled, "I Love Mustard," which goes on for pages about the history of mustard, extols its virtues, and evolves into an ode to his love for it. May I say, I agree?

Mustard can be savory, sweet, spicy, tangy, or salty, and anything you add it to sings a better song. I began experimenting by adding more ingredient twists to my basic mustard recipe in my kitchen in the south of France. So many lavender bushes surrounded my house and snuggled up to the wall beside my kitchen door that lavender inevitably found its way one day into my mustard.

That was my first big leap into mustard making, when I would go outside to gather lavender and make homemade mustard with masses of these aromatic buds added. When it was slathered on bread topped with country pâté it cat-apulted a humble dish into the stratosphere of amazing flavor combinations you never forget. So feel comfortable adding almost anything you can think of to mustard to make it interesting: fruit, honey, spices, beer, wine, fruit juice, port wine, champagne, or whiskey.

The first couple of recipes in this chapter start you off with basic mustards to make at home. The simplest way is to mix American or English mustard powder you buy at the supermarket with some water and vinegar. You can also make it with mustard seeds you grind yourself. Yellow seeds produce a milder mustard while brown or black will produce a stronger mustard.

Basic Yellow Hot Dog Mustard

MAKES 1 CUP

1 cup water
2 ounces yellow mustard powder
1/2 teaspoon ground turmeric
1/4 teaspoon garlic powder

1 1/2 teaspoon fine sea salt
1/8 teaspoon sweet paprika
3 teaspoons distilled white
    vinegar, or more if needed

Combine the water, mustard, turmeric, garlic powder, salt, and paprika in a saucepan over medium heat and cook, whisking frequently and letting it bubble a little, for 13 to 15 minutes or until it thickens. Remove from the heat, whisk in the vinegar, teaspoon by teaspoon, and taste as you go. Add more vinegar by the teaspoon if you like. Cool in the saucepan to room temperature then transfer to glass jar(s) with a screw top and allow to cool to room temperature. Screw on the lids and store in the refrigerator for up to 1 month.

Dijon Mustard

MAKES 1 1/4 CUPS

1/2 cup black or yellow mustard
    seeds (black mustard seeds
    have a stronger flavor)
3/4 cup dry white wine, or
    more if needed

1/4 cup white wine vinegar or
    distilled white vinegar
1/4 teaspoon fine sea salt
2 teaspoons light brown
    sugar, or more if needed
Water, if needed to thin

Grind the mustard seeds in a spice mill or coffee grinder and transfer them to a bowl.

Add the rest of the ingredients, except the water, into the bowl, stir well, cover, and let stand on the counter overnight.

Transfer the mixture to a blender and process until very smooth. Drip in water if it is too thick and blend again. Transfer to glass jar(s) with a screw top and store in the refrigerator for up to 3 days before using to allow the flavors to blend, and store up to 2 months.

Very Strong Whole-Grain Mustard

MAKES 1¾ CUPS

¼ cup yellow mustard seeds
½ cup brown mustard seeds
½ cup apple cider vinegar

½ cup water, white wine, beer, or fruit juice
½ teaspoon fine sea salt

Combine all the ingredients into a quart-size Mason jar, screw on the lid, give it a shake, and let sit on the counter for a couple of days to soften the seeds. If you would like a less bitter mustard, grind the seeds in a spice mill or coffee grinder before combining with the other ingredients in the jar and let it sit on the counter for a couple of days. Or you can grind just half of the seeds.

Transfer the mixture to a blender and process until smooth. Transfer to glass jar(s) with a screw top and store in the refrigerator for up to up to 6 months.

Beer Mustard

MAKES 4 CUPS

1 cup yellow mustard seeds
2 cups dark or amber beer
1 ¼ cups apple cider vinegar
1 teaspoon fine sea salt
6 tablespoons honey

½ cup dark brown sugar
⅛ teaspoon ground cloves
1 teaspoon ground allspice
Water, if needed to thin

Place the mustard seeds into a quart-size Mason jar. Pour in the beer and vinegar, screw on the top, and let sit on the counter for 2 days to soften the seeds.

Combine the salt, honey, brown sugar, cloves, and allspice in a saucepan over medium heat and cook, whisking just until the salt and sugars are dissolved. Remove from the heat and allow to cool to room temperature.

Transfer the mustard seed mixture and the mixture in the saucepan to a food processor or blender and process until it reaches your desired consistency. Add a bit of water if it is too thick. Transfer to glass jar(s) with a screw top and store in the refrigerator for up to 2 months.

Sweet Whiskey Mustard

MAKES 1½ CUPS

1 cup yellow mustard seeds
3 tablespoons whiskey
1 tablespoon water
½ cup distilled white vinegar

2 tablespoons light brown sugar
2 tablespoons honey
¼ teaspoon ground nutmeg
1 teaspoon fine sea salt

Combine the mustard seeds, whiskey, water, and vinegar in a glass bowl, stir, cover, and leave on the counter for 24 hours.

Stir in the brown sugar, honey, nutmeg, and salt. Transfer ⅔ of the mixture to a blender or food processor and process until very smooth. Pour the mixture back into the bowl with the whole mustard seeds and whisk well to combine. Transfer to glass jar(s) with a screw top and store in the refrigerator for up to 2 months.

Yummy Orange Mustard

MAKES 1 CUP

½ cup yellow mustard seeds
1 tablespoon brown mustard seeds
2 organic oranges
3 tablespoons granulated sugar
3 tablespoons light brown sugar

1 teaspoon fine sea salt
⅛ teaspoon ground cloves
7 to 8 tablespoons apple
   cider vinegar, to taste

In a coffee grinder or spice mill, grind the mustard seeds as finely as you can and set aside.

Grate the zest from 1 of the oranges into a bowl. Add the granulated and brown sugars and, with your fingers, rub the zest and sugars together to release the orange oil into the sugars. Alternatively, you can do this in a food processor.

Juice the oranges and pour the juice into a saucepan. Bring to a boil and let it boil down and reduce by half. Pour into the bowl with the sugar mixture.

Add the reserved ground mustard, salt, cloves, and vinegar to the bowl and whisk to combine. It will appear to be too liquid but it will firm up and come together in the refrigerator. Transfer to glass jar(s) with a screw top and store in the refrigerator for up to 2 days before using to allow the flavors to blend, and store up to 2 months.

Chipotle Honey Mustard

MAKES 2 CUPS

½ cup yellow mustard seeds
¼ cup apple cider vinegar
¼ distilled white vinegar
½ cup blond beer, of choice

1 (5-ounce) can chipotle
   peppers in adobo sauce
½ teaspoon fine sea salt
1 red Fresno chile, seeded and diced
5 tablespoons honey

Combine the mustard seeds, vinegars, and beer in a large Mason jar, screw on the top, and allow to sit on the counter for 2 or 3 days to soften the seeds.

Transfer the mixture to a food processor or blender. Add the chipotle peppers and their sauce, salt, Fresno chile, and honey and process until smooth. Taste and adjust seasoning. Transfer to glass jar(s) with a screw top and store in the refrigerator for up to 2 days before using to allow the flavors to blend, and store up to 2 months.

Sweet Apricot Mustard

MAKES 1½ CUPS

½ cup yellow mustard seeds
½ cup dried apricots,
   coarsely chopped, plus
   14 whole dried apricots
½ cup apple cider vinegar

½ cup water
1 teaspoon fine sea salt
6 heaping tablespoons apricot
   preserves, or more as needed

In a large glass jar or bowl, combine the mustard seeds, chopped apricots, vinegar, and water. Give it a good stir, cover, and leave on the kitchen counter for 24 hours for the seeds to absorb the liquid and soften.

Pulse the whole dried apricots in a food processor just until you get small chunks, then transfer to a bowl.

Add the mustard mixture to the food processor (no need to wash), add the salt, and process until you have a smooth mustard. Add the apricot preserves and process again until well combined. Taste and add more preserves if desired. Stir in the apricot chunks. Transfer to glass jar(s) with a screw top and store in the refrigerator for up to 2 months.

Fresh Fig and Port Wine Mustard

MAKES 1½ TO 2 CUPS

6 large fresh ripe figs, washed, stemmed, and quartered
3 tablespoons granulated sugar
3 tablespoons light brown sugar
2 tablespoons white balsamic vinegar

¼ cup port wine
1½ tablespoons mustard powder
½ tablespoon yellow mustard seeds
1 teaspoon ground cinnamon
¼ teaspoon ground cloves
¼ teaspoon fine sea salt

Process the figs in a food processor or blender until smooth.

In a saucepan, combine all the ingredients, except the figs, and cook over medium heat, whisking often, until the sugars dissolve. Lower the heat to low, add the figs, stir, and cook until the mixture thickens. If needed, raise the heat a bit and cook longer until it thickens more to your liking.

Transfer to glass jar(s) with a screw top and allow to cool to room temperature. Screw on the lid and store in the refrigerator for up to 3 weeks. To serve, bring to room temperature.

Flavored Vinegars

VINEGARS TAKE ON jewellike colors when infused with herbs and fruits. I particularly love my recipe for Springtime Pink Chive Blossom Vinegar (page 39) that turns a whimsical pink color and tastes like chives, and my Strawberry Vinegar (page 38) because it conveniently uses up the tops of strawberries, leaving you to enjoy the remaining fruit for another purpose. Any of these make great gifts presented in decorative bottles, especially when you insert a whole branch of an herb or colorful citrus peels inside.

If you are using screw-top glass canning jars to flavor your vinegars, always top with a circle of parchment paper before screwing on the lid so the vinegar does not interact with the lid. If you are using decorative bottles with rubber stoppers, you can skip this step.

Fresh Dill Vinegar

MAKES 2 CUPS

4 stems fresh dill, including the
flowers if you can get them

2 cups distilled white vinegar
or white wine vinegar
¼ teaspoon fine sea salt

Slip the dill stems into a glass jar with a screw top. Add the vinegar and salt. Top with a circle of parchment paper, screw on the top, and let it sit at room temperature for 2 weeks before using.

Strawberry Vinegar

MAKES 2 CUPS

10 to 16 whole strawberries with
their green tops (depending
on the size of the berries)

2 cups distilled white vinegar
or white balsamic vinegar

Cut off the top greens of the strawberries including ½ inch of the fruit, and toss these into 1 or 2 glass jars with screw tops. Save the rest of the strawberries for another use or freeze.

Pour the vinegar over the strawberry tops all the way to the top of the jar(s). Top with circles of parchment paper and screw on the tops. Give them a good shake and store in the refrigerator for 3 days. Taste and if it needs more time to develop the flavors, store for another 3 days before straining out the strawberry tops and transferring the now red vinegar back into the jar(s) or to a decorative bottle. Store in the refrigerator for up to 2 weeks.

STRAWBERRY
VINEGAR

FRESH DILL
VINEGAR

Springtime Pink Chive Blossom Vinegar

MAKES 1 CUP

1 cup distilled white vinegar
5 fresh pink chive blossoms

Pour the vinegar into a glass jar with a screw top. Add the chive blossoms.
Top with a circle of parchment paper and screw on the top. Store in the
refrigerator for at least 4 days before using. The vinegar will be pink and
infused with a lovely chive flavor. Using more than 5 blossoms will make
the vinegar a darker pink and give it a stronger flavor.

Red Pepper Vinegar

MAKES 2 CUPS

2 cups distilled white vinegar
15 black or pink peppercorns
½ medium shallot, minced
2 tablespoons granulated sugar

¼ teaspoon fine sea salt
2 red bell peppers, seeded and
　cut into large chunks

Combine the vinegar, peppercorns, shallot, sugar, and salt in a saucepan
and bring to a boil over medium heat, stirring occasionally, until the sugar is
dissolved. Reduce the heat to maintain a simmer, add the bell peppers, and
cook for 2 minutes. Remove from the heat and pour everything into glass
jar(s) with screw tops.

Allow the vinegar to cool to room temperature. Top with circles of parchment
paper and screw on the tops. Store in a dark place overnight, then strain into
a decorative bottle. The peppers can be reserved to use in salads and the
rest discarded.

Flavored Olive Oils

FLAVORED OILS are fabulous draped or drizzled on or around or over almost any kind of meal you are serving.

Why olive oil and not another neutral oil? You can do that, there's no problem with substituting a neutral oil in these recipes. Using a more neutral oil allows the flavors you are infusing it with to shine. However, if I am making something special, I always use extra-virgin olive oil because I love the flavor. My preference is for Greek or French olive oils.

When using fresh herbs, make sure they are thoroughly dry after you wash them as wet herbs can cause the oil to become cloudy. Use the oils within one week and always store them in the refrigerator as they use fresh produce.

Kalamata Olive Infused Olive Oil

MAKES 1¼ CUPS

1 cup extra-virgin olive oil
½ cup kalamata olives, pitted
   and coarsely chopped

¼ teaspoon fresh thyme leaves
¼ teaspoon fine sea salt

Combine all the ingredients in a small saucepan over medium-low heat and cook, without reaching a simmer, for about 8 minutes. Remove from the heat and allow the mixture to steep for 2 hours. Strain into a decorative bottle with a stopper or into a glass jar with a screw top and seal. Store in the refrigerator for up to 1 week. Bring to room temperature before using.

Emerald Green Basil Oil

MAKES 2 CUPS

1 cup tightly packed
   fresh basil leaves

¼ teaspoon fine sea salt
2 cups extra-virgin olive oil

Pour some water into a mixing bowl and add ice to make an ice bath. Set this aside.

Bring a saucepan of water to a boil. Add the basil leaves and blanch them for about 15 seconds, until the leaves are soft and bright green. Use tongs or a slotted spoon to transfer them to the ice bath and submerge them to stop the cooking process. Transfer the leaves to paper towels and pat dry.

Combine the blanched basil, salt, and oil in a blender or food processor and process until well blended and smooth.

Place a sieve over a bowl and line the sieve with cheesecloth. Pour the mixture into the cheesecloth and let it drip. It's okay to squeeze the cheesecloth to help it drain. If you do not have cheesecloth, strain it through a fine-mesh strainer or paper coffee filter.

Transfer the basil oil to an airtight container and store in the refrigerator for up to 1 week. Bring to room temperature before using.

Pretty Mediterranean Infused Oil

MAKES 1 CUP

1 cup extra-virgin olive oil
¼ cup fresh rosemary needles, cut in half, plus 1 rosemary sprig
1 tablespoon fresh oregano leaves, washed and dried
5 garlic cloves, lightly crushed

¼ teaspoon fine sea salt
½ teaspoon crushed red pepper flakes
1 small red Fresno chile, cut in half, seeds removed

Combine the oil, ¼ cup rosemary, oregano, garlic, salt, and red pepper flakes in a saucepan over medium-low heat, and bring to a gentle simmer. Cook, stirring, until you can smell the aroma of the spices, 2 to 3 minutes. Allow to cool in the saucepan to room temperature.

Slip the whole rosemary sprig and Fresno chile into a bottle that will hold your oil.

Strain the oil into a bowl and discard the spices. Use a funnel to pour the oil into the bottle and seal. Store in the refrigerator for up to 1 week. Bring to room temperature before using.

Hot Jalapeño Oil

MAKES 2 CUPS

2 jalapeño peppers
1 serrano pepper
1 whole garlic bulb
¼ cup fresh cilantro leaves

¼ teaspoon fine sea salt
2 cups extra-virgin olive
    oil or avocado oil

Cut the stem off the peppers and discard. Cut the peppers in half lengthwise and toss them into a large saucepan. Cut the whole garlic bulb in half horizontally and drop into the saucepan.

Add the rest of the ingredients to the saucepan and bring to a strong simmer. Lower the heat to maintain a gentle simmer and cook for 30 minutes.

Remove from the heat and allow the mixture to cool in the saucepan to room temperature. Strain the oil into an airtight container, discard the solids, and store in the refrigerator for up to 1 week. Bring to room temperature before using.

Garlic Chili Oil

MAKES 2 CUPS

2 cups extra-virgin olive oil
8 large garlic cloves, sliced

2 teaspoons crushed red
    pepper flakes
¼ teaspoon fine sea salt

Combine all the ingredients in a saucepan over medium-low heat. Cook, maintaining a low simmer, for 8 minutes. Allow to cool in the saucepan to room temperature. Pour the olive oil mixture into the bottle and seal. The oil can be stored in the refrigerator for up to 1 week. Bring to room temperature before using.

Lemon or Orange Infused Oil

MAKES 1 CUP

1 large organic lemon or orange
1 cup extra-virgin olive oil

¼ teaspoon fine sea salt

Use a vegetable peeler to peel long strips of the citrus rind. Try not to include any of the white pith. Combine the peels, oil, and salt in a saucepan over medium-low heat. Cook only until very warm, without reaching a simmer, about 8 minutes.

Remove from the heat and allow the oil to cool in the saucepan to room temperature. Strain the oil into a bowl and discard the citrus. Pour the citrus-flavored oil into a glass bottle with a rubber stopper or a glass jar with screw top and seal. Store in the refrigerator for up to 1 week. Bring to room temperature before using.

Sun-Dried Tomato and Basil Infused Oil

MAKES 1 CUP

1 cup extra-virgin olive oil
4 store-bought sun-dried tomatoes
   in oil, coarsely chopped
1 teaspoon oil from the jar of
   sun-dried tomatoes
1 large garlic clove, crushed

1 tablespoon dried basil
   or 1 tablespoon minced
   fresh basil leaves

Combine all the ingredients in a small saucepan over medium-low heat and cook, without reaching a simmer, for 10 minutes. Remove from the heat and allow to steep for 2 hours. Strain into a decorative bottle with a stopper or a glass jar with a screw top and seal. Store in the refrigerator for up to 1 week. Bring to room temperature before using.

Bread Dipping Oils

THE BEST OIL to use for bread dipping, in my opinion, is a robustly flavored extra-virgin olive oil. Paired with a fabulous warm crusty bread, it makes an excellent Mediterranean condiment that is packed with flavor and promise for the meal to come.

My recipe for Sun-Dried Tomato Bread Dipping Oil (page 49) will take you back to a romantic dinner in a village piazza in Tuscany. The recipe for my Pesto Bread Dipping Oil (page 48) came from my neighbor in the south of France. And my Provençal Bread Dipping Oil (page 49) is one I made up after picking the last of the summer tomatoes at my house on the Côte d'Azur. It seems as if these dipping oils come with happy memories too.

Balsamic Bread Dipping Oil

MAKES ¾ CUP

½ cup extra-virgin olive oil
3 tablespoons balsamic vinegar
4 large garlic cloves, minced
3 tablespoons minced fresh
  Italian flat-leaf parsley leaves

1 sprig fresh rosemary,
  leaves minced
6 fresh basil leaves, minced
¼ teaspoon crushed red
  pepper flakes
½ teaspoon coarse sea salt flakes

Combine all the ingredients in a bowl and whisk well to combine. Transfer the mixture to a shallow serving bowl or plate.

Pesto Bread Dipping Oil

MAKES ½ CUP

3 tablespoons store-bought pesto
½ cup extra-virgin olive oil
Zest and juice of ½ organic lemon
1 teaspoon dried basil

1 garlic clove, minced
¼ teaspoon coarse sea salt flakes
2 tablespoons grated
  Parmesan cheese

Whisk together the pesto, olive oil, lemon zest and juice, basil, garlic, and salt in a bowl. Transfer the mixture to a shallow serving bowl or plate, then sprinkle the grated cheese on top.

Provençal Bread Dipping Oil

MAKES 1 CUP

1 large ripe tomato, sliced in half
2 tablespoons black olive tapenade
¼ teaspoon coarse sea salt flakes
Freshly ground black
    pepper, to taste
1 garlic clove, minced

1 tablespoon minced
    fresh basil leaves
1 teaspoon dried oregano
2 teaspoons dried basil
½ cup extra-virgin olive oil,
    plus more as needed

Grate the tomato halves into a bowl, using the large holes of a box grater. Add the rest of the ingredients, whisk well, allow to marinate for 1 hour, then serve. Add more olive oil, if needed to thin. Transfer the mixture to a shallow serving bowl or plate.

Sun-Dried Tomato Bread Dipping Oil

MAKES ¾ CUP

½ cup extra-virgin olive oil
¼ cup store-bought sun-dried
    tomatoes in oil, drained, minced
2 large garlic cloves, minced
2 tablespoons minced
    fresh basil leaves

¼ teaspoon fine sea salt
¼ teaspoon crushed red
    pepper flakes (optional)
3 tablespoons grated
    Parmesan cheese

Combine all the ingredients in a bowl and mix well. Allow the mixture to marinate for 1 hour. Transfer the mixture to a shallow serving bowl or plate.

Two-Cheese Bread Dipping Oil

MAKES 1¼ CUP

¼ cup shredded Asiago cheese
¼ cup grated Pecorino
  Romano cheese
2 large garlic cloves, minced
⅛ teaspoon crushed red
  pepper flakes

½ teaspoon coarse sea salt flakes
2 teaspoons dried Italian seasoning
½ cup extra-virgin olive oil,
  or more as desired
1 tablespoon white balsamic vinegar

Whisk together all the ingredients in a bowl. Transfer the mixture to a shallow serving bowl or plate.

Olive and Roasted Garlic Bread Dipping Oil

MAKES 1 CUP

½ cup extra-virgin olive oil,
  plus more as needed
1 whole garlic bulb, sliced
  in half horizontally
6 large green olives,
  pitted and minced
6 kalamata olives, pitted and minced
2 tablespoons minced fresh
  Italian flat-leaf parsley
2 tablespoons finely chopped
  scallion, white part only

1 red Fresno chile, seeded
  and minced
Zest of 1 organic lemon
1 teaspoon Dijon mustard
3 tablespoons grated Parmesan
  or Pecorino Romano cheese
¼ teaspoon fine sea salt flakes
Freshly ground black
  pepper, to taste
3 tablespoons balsamic vinegar

Preheat the oven to 400 degrees F.

Cut a piece of aluminum foil. Drizzle a little oil in the center, place the garlic bulb halves in the oil, drizzle a little more oil over the tops of the garlic, and loosely wrap the garlic in the foil. Place the foil package on a baking sheet and bake for 40 minutes. Open the packet carefully and allow to cool to room temperature.

Squeeze the garlic flesh out of their skins into a bowl. Add the olives, parsley, scallion, red chile, lemon zest, mustard, cheese, salt, pepper, balsamic vinegar, and the ½ cup olive oil. Whisk well to combine and add more of any of the seasonings to taste. Transfer the mixture to a shallow serving bowl or plate.

Restaurant-Style Bread Dipping Oil

MAKES ½ CUP

1 teaspoon onion powder
2 teaspoons garlic powder
1 teaspoon dried rosemary
2 teaspoons dried basil
1 teaspoon dried oregano
2 teaspoons dried parsley
2 tablespoons grated
    Parmesan cheese

Freshly ground black
    pepper, to taste
½ teaspoon coarse sea salt flakes
¼ teaspoon crushed red
    pepper flakes
½ cup extra-virgin olive oil

Combine all the ingredients in a bowl and mix well. Transfer the mixture to a shallow serving bowl or plate.

Vinaigrettes

ALWAYS AN EMULSION of an acid and an oil, and usually three parts oil to one part acid, vinaigrettes can be simply whisked together, vigorously shaken up in a screw-top jar, or come together with an electric beater.

However, one of the best salads I ever had was when a friend drizzled some lemon juice over greens, gently massaged it in, then scattered a generous amount of smoked sea salt over the top and quickly tossed it all together. Only then did she drop in a bit of fruity olive oil, massage again, and finally shave some aged Parmesan over the top. So vinaigrettes can be emulsified, or the ingredients simply added right onto a salad and tossed by hand or massaged into the greens.

Basic French Vinaigrette

MAKES 1 CUP

¼ cup freshly squeezed
    lemon juice or vinegar
¼ teaspoon fine sea salt
½ teaspoon Dijon mustard
¾ cup extra-virgin olive oil

Whisk together all the
ingredients in a bowl.

Italian Vinaigrette

MAKES 1 CUP

¼ cup red wine vinegar
3 garlic cloves, peeled and pressed
½ teaspoon dried oregano or
    Italian seasoning blend
¼ teaspoon fine sea salt

½ teaspoon Dijon mustard
¾ cup extra-virgin olive oil

Whisk together all the
ingredients in a bowl.

Greek Vinaigrette

MAKES 1 CUP

¼ cup red wine vinegar or
    white wine vinegar
1 tablespoon freshly
    squeezed lemon juice
½ teaspoon Dijon mustard
1 garlic clove, peeled and pressed

¼ teaspoon fine sea salt
¼ teaspoon dried oregano
¾ cup extra-virgin olive oil
1 tablespoon plain Greek yogurt
1 tablespoon crumbled feta
    cheese (optional)

Whisk together all the ingredients in a bowl.

Balsamic Vinaigrette

MAKES 1 CUP

¾ cup extra-virgin olive oil
¼ cup balsamic vinegar
¼ teaspoon fine sea salt
1 teaspoon Dijon mustard
1 garlic clove, sliced (optional)

Whisk together all the ingredients in a bowl.

Fresh Lemon Vinaigrette

MAKES 1 CUP

¾ cup extra-virgin olive oil
¼ cup freshly squeezed lemon juice
¼ teaspoon fine sea salt
1 teaspoon Dijon mustard

1 garlic clove, minced
1 tablespoon grated
   Parmesan cheese

Whisk together all the ingredients in a bowl.

Lemon-Honey Vinaigrette

MAKES 1 CUP

Zest and juice of 1 ½ organic lemons
1 teaspoon Dijon mustard
¼ teaspoon fine sea salt

1 tablespoon honey
¾ cup extra-virgin olive
   oil or avocado oil

Whisk together all the ingredients in a bowl.

White Miso Vinaigrette

MAKES 1 CUP

1 tablespoon white miso paste
2 tablespoons freshly
squeezed lemon juice
2 tablespoons rice vinegar

¾ cup extra-virgin olive oil

Whisk together all the
ingredients in a bowl.

Chili Crisp Vinaigrette

MAKES 1 CUP

1 tablespoon chili crisp
¼ cup rice vinegar
⅔ cup avocado oil
1 tablespoon soy sauce

2 teaspoons honey
1 teaspoon Dijon mustard
2 teaspoons sesame oil
1 scallion, sliced very thin

Whisk together the chili crisp, vinegar, oil, soy sauce, honey, mustard, and
sesame oil in a bowl. Add the scallion and stir.

Very Olive Vinaigrette

MAKES 1 CUP

¾ cup extra-virgin olive oil
¼ cup white wine or distilled
white vinegar
1 teaspoon honey

2 large garlic cloves, sliced
1 teaspoon Dijon mustard
6 kalamata or cured black
olives, pitted

Combine all the ingredients in a blender or food processor and process until
smooth. Taste and adjust seasonings, if desired.

Basil Vinaigrette

MAKES 1½ CUPS

2 large garlic cloves, peeled
2 cups tightly packed
  fresh basil leaves
3 tablespoons distilled white
  vinegar or white wine vinegar

1 teaspoon Dijon mustard
¼ teaspoon fine sea salt
1 cup extra-virgin olive oil

Combine all the ingredients in a blender or food processor and process until smooth. Use or store in a jar with a screw top in the refrigerator up to 5 days.

Tequila, Lime, and Cilantro Vinaigrette

MAKES 1¼ CUPS

1 garlic clove, peeled
¼ cup tightly packed fresh
  cilantro leaves
¼ cup freshly squeezed lime juice
¼ teaspoon fine sea salt

1 tablespoon honey
2 tablespoons tequila
1 tablespoon mayonnaise
  or sour cream
½ cup extra-virgin olive oil

Combine the garlic, cilantro, lime juice, salt, honey, tequila, and mayonnaise in a blender or food processor and process until smooth. With the machine running, stream in the olive oil and process until well combined.

Fresh Mango-Orange Vinaigrette

MAKES 1¼ CUPS

1 large ripe mango, diced
¼ cup fresh orange juice
¼ cup rice vinegar, white balsamic, or apple cider vinegar, plus more if needed
¾ cup extra-virgin olive oil, plus more if needed

1 tablespoon honey
1 teaspoon Dijon mustard
¼ teaspoon fine sea salt
¼ teaspoon crushed red pepper flakes, optional

Combine all the ingredients in a blender or food processor and process until smooth. Add a bit of oil or vinegar to thin if needed.

Fig Vinaigrette

MAKES ½ CUP

¼ cup extra-virgin olive oil
1 teaspoon Dijon mustard
2 tablespoons balsamic vinegar or white balsamic vinegar

1 teaspoon honey
½ teaspoon fine sea salt
3 fresh ripe figs, peeled and sliced, or 2 tablespoons fig jam

Combine all the ingredients in a food processor and process until well combined. Taste and adjust seasonings, if desired. Add a bit of water, if needed and process to thin it out as it may depend on the size of your figs.

Blueberry Basil Vinaigrette

MAKES 1¼ CUPS

½ cup fresh blueberries
2 tablespoons distilled white vinegar
2 teaspoons Dijon mustard
¼ teaspoon fine sea salt
1 teaspoon sugar

½ shallot, chopped
¼ cup tightly packed
   fresh basil leaves
½ cup extra-virgin olive oil,
   plus more if needed

Combine all the ingredients in a blender and process until smooth. Thin it out with a bit more oil, if needed.

Raspberry Jam Vinaigrette

MAKES ½ CUP

1½ teaspoons Dijon mustard
¼ teaspoon fine sea salt
3 tablespoons raspberry jam

2 tablespoons distilled white vinegar
⅓ cup extra-virgin olive oil

Whisk together all the ingredients in a bowl. Taste and adjust seasonings, if desired.

Salad Dressings

LET'S FACE IT. Salad greens are bland and need a killer vinaigrette or creamy dressing to bring them to life. I always make my own dressings, knowing that almost all bottled dressings have shelf-life enhancers and added things I really don't want on my salad. I just want real.

You can't beat a homemade dressing like My Grandmother's Ranch Dressing (page 64), or my recipe for the Restaurant-Style Carrot-Ginger Dressing (page 62) that you find on salads in Japanese restaurants. The next time you serve a wedge, make my Thousand Island Dressing (page 63) to liberally drape over it.

Green Goddess Dressing

MAKES 1½ CUPS

¾ cup mayonnaise
¼ cup buttermilk
½ cup tightly packed
    fresh basil leaves
1 scallion, trimmed, cut in quarters
⅓ cup tightly packed fresh Italian
    flat-leaf parsley leaves

2 teaspoons freshly
    squeezed lemon juice
2 cloves garlic, peeled
2 oil-packed anchovy fillets
Fine sea salt, if needed

Combine all the ingredients in a food processor and process until smooth.
Taste and add salt if desired. Chill until ready to use.

Restaurant-Style Carrot-Ginger Dressing

MAKES 1¼ CUPS

1 medium carrot, peeled,
    cut in 1-inch pieces
¼ small red onion
1 (½-inch) knob fresh ginger,
    peeled and coarsely chopped
1 tablespoon plus 1 teaspoon
    mellow white miso

3 teaspoons toasted sesame oil
1 tablespoon granulated sugar
½ cup rice vinegar
1 tablespoon soy sauce
½ cup avocado or other neutral oil

Combine all the ingredients in a food
processor and process until smooth.
Depending on the size of your carrot,
the mixture may be too thick and
you can add a bit of water to thin the
dressing out. Chill until ready to use.

Creamy Asian Peanut Dressing

MAKES 1¼ CUPS

½ cup unsalted peanuts
3 garlic cloves
4 slices peeled fresh ginger,
    about ¼-inch thick
5 tablespoons creamy peanut butter
2 tablespoons avocado oil or
    neutral oil, plus more if needed

3 tablespoons hoisin sauce
2 teaspoons soy sauce
3 teaspoons sesame oil
⅓ cup rice vinegar
2 teaspoons granulated sugar
Dash of hot sauce, optional

In a food processor, pulse the peanuts until finely chopped. Transfer to a small bowl.

Combine all the rest of the ingredients into the food processor and process until smooth. Add a bit more oil if it is too thick. Stir in the chopped peanuts. Transfer to a serving bowl.

Thousand Island Dressing

MAKES 1½ CUPS

1 cup mayonnaise
¼ cup plus 1 tablespoon ketchup
Zest and juice of 1 organic lemon
¼ teaspoon fine sea salt
1 teaspoon finely chopped capers
1 tablespoon sweet pickle relish

1 tablespoon minced fresh chives
1 tablespoon minced fresh Italian
    flat-leaf parsley leaves
1 hard-boiled egg, minced

Combine the mayonnaise, ketchup, lemon zest, 2 teaspoons lemon juice, salt, capers, relish, chives, and parsley into a bowl and whisk to combine. Stir in the minced egg and chill until ready to use.

My Grandmother's Ranch Dressing

MAKES 1½ CUPS

½ cup plain full-fat Greek yogurt
1 teaspoon fine sea salt
¾ cup buttermilk, plus
    more if needed
½ cup mayonnaise
Juice of ½ lemon
2 tablespoons distilled white vinegar
2 cloves garlic, peeled and sliced
2 tablespoons chopped fresh
    Italian flat-leaf parsley

1 tablespoon chopped
    fresh dill fronds
2 tablespoons chopped fresh chives
Coarsely ground black pepper,
    to taste

Combine all the ingredients in a blender and process until smooth. Add a bit more buttermilk if needed to thin it out.

Creamy Blue Cheese Dressing

MAKES 1½ CUPS

¼ pound wedge blue cheese or
    Gorgonzola (not crumbles)
½ cup mayonnaise
½ cup plain full-fat Greek yogurt
3 garlic cloves, sliced

1 tablespoon capers, drained
¼ teaspoon fine sea salt
2 tablespoons white wine or
    distilled white vinegar
2 tablespoons extra-virgin olive oil

Break the cheese in pieces and place into a food processor. Add the rest of the ingredients and process until smooth, scraping down the sides of the food processor a couple of times. Taste and adjust seasoning if needed.

Poppyseed Dressing

MAKES ¾ CUP

½ cup plain full-fat Greek yogurt
2 tablespoons extra-virgin olive oil
2 tablespoons distilled white vinegar
1 tablespoon honey
1 tablespoon maple syrup
½ teaspoon Dijon mustard

2 tablespoons poppy seeds
½ teaspoon fine sea salt

Whisk the ingredients together in a bowl. Chill until ready to use.

Creamy Coleslaw Dressing

MAKES 2¼ CUPS

½ cup sour cream
½ cup mayonnaise
1 cup plain full-fat Greek yogurt
2 tablespoons Dijon mustard
¼ cup plus 2 tablespoons
    white balsamic vinegar

½ cup granulated sugar
¼ cup honey
1 teaspoon fine sea salt

Whisk together all the ingredients in a bowl. Chill until ready to use.

Miso Poke Bowl Dressing

MAKES ⅔ CUP

2 tablespoons mellow white miso
1 (2-inch) knob fresh ginger,
    peeled, sliced
1 garlic clove, sliced
1 tablespoon honey
2 teaspoons sesame oil
4 tablespoons extra-virgin olive oil

2 tablespoons mirin
1 tablespoon soy sauce
Zest and juice of ½ organic lime

Combine all the ingredients in a food processor and process until smooth.

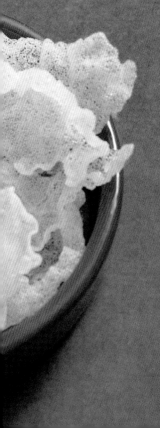

Salad Toppers

THIS IS THE SURPRISE ELEMENT that takes a salad over the top. After dressing it, place small bowls of these on your condiment board next to the big salad bowl for topping.

Candied Walnuts or Pecans

MAKES 1 CUP

1 cup walnut or pecan halves
1 tablespoon salted butter
¼ cup granulated sugar

½ teaspoon ground cinnamon
¼ teaspoon ground nutmeg
¼ teaspoon coarse sea salt

Lay out a large piece of parchment paper on the kitchen counter.

In a large nonstick skillet, place all the ingredients in separate piles in the skillet, and cook over medium heat, until the sugar and butter have melted. While the butter and sugar melt on their own, the nuts will toast.

Once the butter and sugar have melted, constantly stir the nuts in the melted butter until they are evenly coated, about 5 minutes.

Transfer the nuts to the parchment paper and, using tongs or two forks, separate them and spread them out to cool for about 10 minutes. Serve them in a bowl.

Baked Cheese Crisp Shards

4 ounces freshly grated Parmesan
   cheese (grate it yourself, don't
   use preshredded or grated
   cheese, which has additives)

Garlic powder or everything
   bagel seasoning
Freshly ground black pepper

Preheat the oven to 400 degrees F. Line a baking sheet with parchment paper or use a silicone baking sheet.

Spread out the cheese on the baking sheet and lightly pat it down into a large rectangle. Sprinkle garlic powder and pepper over the top. Bake for 6 to 7 minutes, or until golden and crisp.

Remove from the oven and allow the cheese crisp to come to room temperature on the baking sheet. Cut the crisp into your desired shapes with a pizza cutter or sharp knife or break it up with your hands. Spread the pieces out on paper towels to absorb any oil. Serve on a plate or in a shallow bowl.

Fried-Rice Paper Puffs

Enough sunflower oil or olive oil to fill ½ inch up the
    sides of a skillet or small saucepan
Rice paper wrappers, made from 100 percent rice flour, cut into
    quarters or eighths with scissors or break up using your hands
Fine sea salt

Heat the oil in a skillet or small saucepan to 380 degrees F. If you don't have a thermometer, heat the oil then test it with tiny pieces of rice paper wrappers until you see that they swell up and turn opaque white.

Drop in the pieces of rice paper. They will curl up into puffs in about 3 seconds. Use a slotted spoon or tongs to transfer them to paper towels. Toss them with salt and serve.

You can use any seasonings you like on them. Try Old Bay or lemon pepper or seasoning salt or cracked pepper. Pile attractively into a bowl or plate to scatter like croutons across salads. You can also fill them with sour cream and caviar or guacamole and offer as a passed hors d'oeuvre.

Marinated Cheese with Peppercorns

MAKES 2 CUPS

OPTION 1

2 teaspoons thyme leaves

1 heaping teaspoon mixed color (red, green, white, black) whole peppercorns

8 ounces Manchego cheese, cut into ½-inch dice

8 ounces fresh goat cheese, rolled into small ½-inch balls

1 cup extra-virgin olive oil, plus more as needed

2 bay leaves

½ teaspoon fine sea salt

½ teaspoon freshly ground black pepper

Combine the thyme, peppercorns, and cheeses into a bowl and set aside.

In a saucepan over medium heat, combine the oil, bay leaves, and salt and bring to a simmer. Cook for 2 minutes. Transfer the bay leaves to 1 or 2 jars with screw tops. Take the saucepan off the heat and whisk in the pepper.

Pour the mixture over the cheese mixture in the bowl and mix gently with a spoon. Transfer everything to the glass jar(s) and top up with enough olive oil to cover the cheese. Seal with the tops and allow cheeses to marinate in the refrigerator for 24 hours.

Remove the jar(s) from the refrigerator and allow to stand at room temperature for 1 hour, or until the olive oil becomes liquid, before serving.

OPTION 2

1 organic lemon

7 ounces Greek or French feta cheese, cut into ½-inch dice

2 teaspoons herbes de Provence

2 teaspoons black or mixed-color peppercorns

¼ teaspoon crushed red pepper flakes

¼ teaspoon fine sea salt

1 cup extra-virgin olive oil, plus more if needed

Grate enough zest from the lemon to make ½ teaspoon. Cut the lemon in half and juice 1 of the halves (about 1 teaspoon). Cut 4 thin slices from the remaining half lemon.

Put the slices of lemon in jar(s) with a screw top. Combine the lemon zest, feta, herbes de Provence, peppercorns, and pepper flakes in a bowl.

In a small bowl, mix together the salt and oil. Pour the mixture over the cheese mixture and gently stir to coat. Transfer the cheese and oil to jar(s), top with enough olive oil to cover the cheese, and screw on the lid(s). Refrigerate for 24 hours. Allow to come to room temperature for at least 1 hour, or until the oil becomes liquid, before serving.

Toasted Seasoned Breadcrumbs (Pangrattoto)

MAKES 1¼ CUPS

3 tablespoons extra-virgin olive oil
1 tablespoon unsalted butter
4 large garlic cloves, minced
⅛ teaspoon fine sea salt, plus more if needed
⅔ cup store-bought breadcrumbs

¼ teaspoon crushed red pepper flakes
¼ cup freshly grated Pecorino Romano cheese
½ cup minced fresh Italian flat-leaf parsley or basil or thyme leaves, minced

Combine the oil, butter, garlic, and salt in a skillet over low heat and heat until the oil is hot. Add the breadcrumbs, pepper flakes, cheese, and parsley and cook until the breadcrumbs become golden, about 5 minutes. Taste and add more salt if desired. Transfer to a small serving bowl.

Salts and Seasonings

HUGE COMPANIES around the world process and sell generic sea salt on a large scale, producing vast quantities that require industrial methods. This includes kosher salt because it is chemically refined in large factories and stripped of its naturally occurring minerals. In some cases, it may contain anticaking agents. Because of this, I choose not to use them. I also choose not to use regular, iodized, heavily processed table salt because of the additives used that can include calcium aluminosilicate, calcium carbonate, fatty acid salts, and magnesium carbonate, among others.

Instead, I prefer to support hand-harvested, small-batch salt farmers. For me, their unrefined sea salt tastes better, so if I am going to cook I want to use the very best quality I can find. It is more expensive than mass-market salt, but it is worth every penny in my opinion. Because sea salts from small sea salt farmers are laboriously gathered by evaporation from the ocean or salt springs in a complicated ballet of coordination between weather, mother nature, hard work, and luck, it is an expensive operation to perform.

I also treasure that each and every natural small-scale salt, amazingly, tastes different and has different levels of saltiness and texture and color. And that's half the fun. See page 12 for some of my favorite store-bought salts that I keep in my pantry.

Besides my love of the incredible varieties and flavors of salts, I also love making seasonings and flavored salts with them. I got my first exposure

Bacon Salt

MAKES ¾ CUP

8 strips bacon
2 teaspoons smoked paprika
2 teaspoons sweet paprika
¾ cup coarse or fine sea salt

½ teaspoon freshly ground
 black pepper
1 teaspoon light brown sugar

In a skillet over medium-high heat, cook the bacon until it is very crispy, 4 to 5 minutes per side. Let drain and cool to room temperature on paper towels.

Break up the bacon with your hands, place it in a food processor, and pulse until finely chopped. Add the rest of the ingredients and process until it has a texture like fine salt. Store the salt in a glass jar with a screw top and refrigerate for up to 2 weeks.

Sriracha Salt

MAKES ½ CUP

½ cup coarse salt, fine sea salt, or Himalayan pink salt
1½ tablespoons sriracha, or more as needed

Preheat the oven to 300 degrees F. Line a baking sheet with parchment paper.

Combine the ingredients in a bowl and mix well. Spread out the mixture on the parchment-lined baking sheet. When the oven reaches 300 degrees F, turn it off, put the baking sheet into the oven, close the door, and leave for 5 hours or overnight to dry out. Store the salt in a glass jar with a screw top in the refrigerator for up to 2 months.

Flavored Sugars

FLAVORED SUGARS often impart stronger flavors than adding
the ingredients separately. When you whiz up fresh lemon peel in
a food processor with sugar then allow it to sit for an hour
or so, the oil from the lemon peel permeates the sugar,
resulting in a more pronounced tangy lemony sugar.

You can make stunningly beautiful colored sugars
simply by using freeze-dried fruits like strawberries, blueberries, or pineapple that are easily
available at many grocery stores or online. Whiz
them into a powder and then mix with sugar. Try
my Bright Pink Strawberry Sugar (page 82)
recipe or Blue Blueberry Sugar (page 82) recipe at
your next brunch. They are beautiful and will be a total
surprise for your guests.

Blue Blueberry Sugar

MAKES 1¼ CUPS

½ cup freeze-dried blueberries
1 cup granulated sugar

¼ teaspoon water

Line a baking sheet with parchment paper.

In a coffee grinder, spice grinder, or food processor, process the dried blueberries until finely ground into powder. Transfer the ground blueberries to a bowl and add the sugar and water. Use your hands to rub the blueberry powder and sugar together and to press out any lumps.

Spread out the mixture on the parchment-lined baking sheet and let dry for 3 hours. Transfer to an airtight container and store for up to 5 months.

Bright Pink Strawberry Sugar

MAKES 1¼ CUP

½ cup freeze-dried strawberries
1 cup granulated sugar
¼ teaspoon water

Line a baking sheet with parchment paper.

In a coffee grinder or spice mill, process the dried strawberries until finely ground into a powder. Transfer the ground strawberries to a bowl and add the sugar and water. Use your hands to rub the strawberry powder and sugar together and press out any lumps.

Spread out the mixture on the parchment-lined baking sheet and let dry for 3 hours or until thoroughly dry. Transfer to an airtight container and store for up to 5 months.

Bright Pink Mini Sugar Cubes

You will need a silicone mini ice cube tray to make these adorable mini pink strawberry sugar cubes.

Make the recipe above for Bright Pink Strawberry Sugar. Pack the mixture tightly into the silicone mini ice cube tray. Let dry overnight before popping them out of the mold. Store in an airtight container for up to 5 months.

Lemon or Lime Sugar

MAKES 1 CUP

1 cup granulated sugar
2 tablespoons organic
    lemon or lime zest

Combine all the ingredients in a bowl. Use your fingers to rub the mixture until the oil releases from the zest. Use right away and, if needed, store in an airtight container in the refrigerator for up to 3 days.

Minty Green Sugar

MAKES 1¼ CUPS

½ cup tightly packed fresh
    mint or spearmint leaves
1 cup granulated sugar

Combine all the ingredients in a food processor and pulse until the mint is finely ground into the sugar. Store in a glass jar with a screw top and refrigerate up to 3 days.

Vanilla Bean and Cardamom Sugar

MAKES 1 CUP

1 vanilla bean, cut into pieces
Seeds from 10 cardamom pods

1 cup granulated sugar

Combine the vanilla bean, cardamom seeds, and ¼ cup of sugar in a food processor and process until the vanilla and seeds are finely chopped. Add the remaining ¾ cup of sugar and process for 60 seconds. Store the sugar in a glass jar with a screw top for 1 week before using.

Coffee Lover's Sugar

MAKES 1 CUP

2 tablespoons coffee beans or
    instant espresso powder
1 cup granulated sugar
2 teaspoons water

Line a baking sheet with parchment paper.

In a coffee grinder or spice mill, grind the coffee beans until very finely ground, as you would when making fresh coffee in the morning. Transfer to a bowl. Add the sugar and water and whisk until very well combined. Using your hands, squeeze and rub the mixture for about 30 seconds. It will turn a dark color.

Spread out the mixture onto the parchment-lined baking sheet and let dry for 24 hours.

Transfer to a bowl and whisk to break up any lumps. Store the sugar in a jar with a screw top.

Coffee Lover's Mini Sugar Cubes

You will need a silicone mini ice cube tray to make adorable mini sugar-coffee cubes.

Make the recipe above for Coffee Lover's Sugar. Pack the mixture tightly into the silicone mini ice cube tray. Let dry for 24 hours before popping them out of the mold. Store the sugar cubes in a jar with a screw top.

Fragrant Lavender Sugar

MAKES 2 CUPS

2 tablespoons edible dried
   lavender flowers
2 cups granulated sugar

Using a mortar and pestle, a spice mill, or a coffee grinder, pulverize the flowers. Transfer the ground lavender to a bowl and whisk in the sugar. Store the sugar in a glass jar with a screw top up to 5 months.

Cinnamon Sugar

MAKES 1 CUP

¼ cup ground cinnamon
½ cup granulated sugar
½ cup light brown or
   turbinado sugar
1 cinnamon stick, broken in half

Whisk together the cinnamon and sugars in a bowl. Transfer to a glass jar with a screw top. Slip in the cinnamon stick halves, screw on the lid, and let sit overnight before using.

Tropical Coconut and Mango Sugar

MAKES 2¾ CUPS

½ cup freeze-dried coconut
½ cup freeze-dried mango

2 cups granulated sugar
2 teaspoons water

Line a baking sheet with parchment paper.

Combine the dried coconut and mango in a spice mill or coffee grinder and process until a fine powder. Transfer the mixture to a bowl. Add the sugar and water and use your hands to rub the fruit powder, sugar, and water together and press out any lumps. Spread out the mixture on the parchment-lined baking sheet and let dry for 3 hours before using. Store the sugar in a glass jar with a screw top for up to 5 months.

Spiced Sugar

MAKES 1 CUP

1 cup granulated sugar
2 vanilla beans
1 tablespoon ground cinnamon

2 teaspoons ground cardamom
½ teaspoon Chinese five-
    spice powder

Pour the sugar into a bowl.

Cut the vanilla beans in half vertically and scrape out the seeds into the sugar. Cut the remaining pods in half and reserve.

Add the rest of the ingredients to the sugar and whisk well to combine. Transfer the mixture to a glass jar with a screw top, slip the reserved vanilla pod pieces into the sugar in the jar, and screw on the lid.

Holiday Orange Rum Sugar

MAKES 1 CUP

1 cup granulated sugar or
    unbleached cane sugar
Zest of 1 organic orange,
    plus 1 teaspoon juice
½ teaspoon vanilla extract

¼ teaspoon ground cinnamon
¼ teaspoon ground nutmeg
⅛ teaspoon ground cloves
2 teaspoons dark rum

Preheat the oven to 170 degrees F. Line a baking sheet with parchment paper.

Combine all the ingredients in a bowl and stir to combine or use your fingers to massage all the ingredients together.

Spread out the mixture on the parchment-lined baking sheet and bake for 15 minutes. Stir the mixture and spread it out again, then bake for another 20 minutes.

Let cool to room temperature. Break up the mixture with a fork and then transfer to a glass jar with a screw top.

Rosemary Sugar

MAKES 1 CUP

1 cup granulated sugar
3 tablespoons finely minced rosemary
¼ teaspoon fine sea salt

Combine all the ingredients in a bowl. Using your fingers, rub the rosemary into the sugar and salt to release the oils or process the ingredients in a food processor. Store the sugar in a glass jar with a screw top for 1 week before using, and then for up to 2 months.

Butters

ONCE A BUTTER LOVER, always a searcher for the perfect butter. I make my own most of the time in small batches because it is so easy and fast. Then I can leave it as is or paddle in fresh fruit, herbs, or spices, and make it salty or sweet.

I often serve a couple of my own creations alongside great store-bought butter I may have been able to find, for a fun taste test. So use either homemade from the recipes below or use top quality store-bought butter.

Try my recipe for Shrimp or Lobster Butter (page 95) smeared on a warm bagel, scoop my Maple-Bacon Butter (page 95) onto pancakes, or put a chunk of my colorful Spicy Cowboy Butter (page 92) on top of grilled seafood or steaks.

But first, let's make the basic butter recipe, because it's the best.

Basic Homemade Butter

MAKES 1 CUP

2 cups high-quality heavy cream (organic and grass-fed if possible), room temperature

Pour the cream into a stand mixer (I use a KitchenAid) and beat on high using the whisk attachment.

Beat past the point of whipped cream and scrape down the sides with a spatula. Drape a towel over the bowl to keep the liquid whey from splashing out and begin beating again. When you hear a slapping noise, it is ready. It means the butter has separated from the liquid. This should take about 13 minutes. Alternatively, you can process the cream in a food processor for about 10 minutes.

Strain the liquid into a bowl and scoop the butter into a sieve to drain. I keep the nutritious liquid whey for another use like adding to my dog's water bowl or for fertilizing my plants.

Use your hands to form the butter solids into a ball and run it under cold water to rinse it off. This is sweet butter. If you want to add salt at this point, simply sprinkle the butter with salt (I use crunchy coarse sea salt flakes) and mix it all up with your hands or a rubber spatula.

Either transfer the butter to a ramekin for serving or wrap it in parchment paper and form it into a log. Store in the refrigerator for up to 3 weeks.

MAPLE-BACON BUTTER

FRESH HERBS AND SEA SALT BUTTER

CINNAMON ROLL BUTTER

SPICY COWBOY BUTTER

Fresh Herbs and Sea Salt Butter

MAKES 1 CUP

1 cup (2 sticks) unsalted
   butter, softened
¼ teaspoon garlic powder (optional)

4 tablespoons minced fresh herbs,
   such as rosemary, chives, parsley,
   thyme, or any from your garden
½ teaspoon coarse sea salt flakes

Beat the butter in a bowl with an electric hand mixer until light and fluffy. Add the garlic powder and beat to combine. Fold in the herbs and coarse sea salt flakes with a spoon.

Either transfer the butter to a ramekin for serving or wrap it in parchment paper and form it into a log. Refrigerate for a few hours to develop the flavors. Store in the refrigerator for up to 3 weeks.

Green Chive and Garlic Butter

MAKES 1 CUP

2 garlic cloves, peeled
¼ cup firmly packed coarsely
   chopped chives

1 teaspoon fine sea salt
1 cup (2 sticks) unsalted
   butter, softened

With a food processor running, drop in the garlic and process until it is finely minced. Add the rest of the ingredients and process until smooth.

Either transfer the butter to a ramekin for serving or wrap it in parchment paper and form it into a log. Refrigerate for a few hours to develop the flavors. Store in the refrigerator for up to 3 weeks.

Avocado Butter

MAKES 1½ CUPS

1 ripe avocado, pitted and peeled
Juice of ½ lemon
1 cup (2 sticks) unsalted
    butter, softened

2 teaspoons fresh thyme leaves
¼ teaspoon coarse sea salt flakes
1 garlic clove, peeled and cut in half

Combine all the ingredients in a food processor and process until very smooth and spreadable.

Either transfer the butter to a ramekin for serving or wrap it in parchment paper and form it into a log. Refrigerate for a few hours to develop the flavors. Store in the refrigerator for up to 3 days.

Spicy Cowboy Butter

MAKES 1 CUP

1 cup (2 sticks) unsalted
    butter, softened
1 tablespoon plus 1 teaspoon
    Dijon mustard
1 teaspoon smoked or sweet paprika
½ teaspoon crushed red
    pepper flakes
½ teaspoon fine sea salt

Zest of 1 organic lemon
1 tablespoon coarsely
    chopped fresh chives
2 tablespoons coarsely chopped
    fresh Italian flat-leaf parsley
1 tablespoon fresh thyme leaves
3 large garlic cloves, sliced

Combine all the ingredients in a food processor and pulse until spreadable. Either transfer the butter to a ramekin for serving or wrap it in parchment paper and form it into a log.

Refrigerate for a few hours to develop the flavors. Store in the refrigerator for up to 1 week.

Lime-Chili Butter

MAKES ½ CUP

½ cup (1 stick) unsalted
    butter, softened
1 tablespoon minced fresh
    cilantro leaves
¼ teaspoon fine sea salt,
    plus more if needed

Zest and juice of 1 organic lime
1 teaspoon Worcestershire sauce
½ teaspoon chili crisp, crispy
    bits only, or 1 minced
    small red Fresno chile

Combine all the ingredients in a bowl and beat with an electric hand mixer until very well blended. Add a little more salt, if needed.

Either transfer the butter to a ramekin for serving or wrap it in parchment paper and form it into a log. Refrigerate for a few hours to develop the flavors. Store in the refrigerator for up to 1 week.

Black Olive Butter

MAKES ⅔ CUP

½ cup (1 stick) unsalted
    butter, softened
⅓ cup kalamata or oil-
    cured olives, pitted

2 garlic cloves, sliced
2 anchovy fillets
¼ cup fresh Italian flat-
    leaf parsley leaves

Combine all the ingredients in a food processor or mini food processor and pulse until well combined but there are still pieces of olives.

Either transfer the butter to a ramekin for serving or wrap it in parchment paper and form it into a log. Refrigerate for a few hours to develop the flavors. Store in the refrigerator for up to 1 week.

Smoky Chipotle Butter

MAKES ½ CUP

½ cup (1 stick) salted
 butter, softened
¼ teaspoon smoked paprika
1 canned chipotle pepper in
 adobo sauce, finely chopped

1 tablespoon of the adobo
 sauce from the can
2 teaspoons freshly
 squeezed lime juice
1 tablespoon minced fresh
 cilantro leaves

Combine the butter and paprika in a bowl and beat with an electric hand mixer until light and fluffy. Add the remaining ingredients and beat again until fluffy and well combined.

Either transfer the butter to a ramekin for serving or wrap it in parchment paper and form it into a log. Refrigerate for a few hours to develop the flavors. Store in the refrigerator for up to 2 weeks.

Anchovy-Garlic Butter

MAKES ½ CUP

½ cup (1 stick) unsalted
 butter, softened
2 teaspoons anchovy paste
2 anchovy fillets, drained,
 finely chopped

½ teaspoon freshly
 squeezed lemon juice
2 garlic cloves, pressed

Combine all the ingredients in a bowl and beat with an electric hand mixer until very well blended.

Either transfer the butter to a ramekin for serving or wrap it in parchment paper and form it into a log. Refrigerate for a few hours to develop the flavors. Store in the refrigerator for up to 2 weeks.

Shrimp or Lobster Butter

MAKES 1½ CUPS

1 cup coarsely chopped cooked
   shrimp or lobster
½ cup (1 stick) salted
   butter, softened

1 tablespoon fresh dill fronds,
   plus more if needed
1 garlic clove, minced (optional)

Combine the ingredients in a blender or food processor and process until well mixed. Either transfer the butter to a ramekin for serving or wrap it in parchment paper and form it into a log. Refrigerate for a few hours to develop the flavors. Store in the refrigerator for up to 4 days.

Maple-Bacon Butter

MAKES 1¼ CUPS

5 slices of bacon
1 cup (2 sticks) unsalted
   butter, softened

3 tablespoons maple syrup
1 tablespoon light brown sugar

Cook the bacon until thoroughly crispy. Transfer to paper towels to drain then finely chop by hand or in a food processor.

Beat the butter in a bowl with an electric hand mixer until light and fluffy. Add the maple syrup and brown sugar and beat to incorporate. Fold in the chopped bacon. Either transfer the butter to a ramekin for serving or wrap it in parchment paper and form it into a log. Refrigerate for a few hours to develop the flavors. Store in the refrigerator for up to 2 weeks.

Brown Sugar and Jalapeño Butter

MAKES ½ CUP

½ cup (1 stick) salted
  butter, softened
2 tablespoons dark brown sugar

¼ teaspoon smoked paprika
1 small jalapeño pepper, minced

Combine all the ingredients in a bowl and beat with an electric hand mixer until creamy and fluffy.

Transfer, either to a ramekin to serve, or wrap the butter in parchment paper and form into a log. Refrigerate for a few hours to develop the flavors. Store in the refrigerator for up to 2 months.

Cinnamon Roll Butter

MAKES ½ CUP

½ cup (1 stick) unsalted
  butter, softened

1 ½ tablespoons honey
2 teaspoons ground cinnamon

Beat all the ingredients together in a bowl with an electric hand mixer. Spoon the mixture into a serving container or bowl.

Orange Marmalade Butter

MAKES ½ CUP

½ cup (1 stick) unsalted
  butter, softened
2 tablespoons thick-cut
  orange marmalade

½ teaspoon vanilla extract
⅛ teaspoon fine sea salt

Beat the ingredients together in a bowl with an electric hand mixer until well mixed. Transfer, either to a ramekin to serve, or wrap the butter in parchment paper and form into a log. Refrigerate until ready to use.

Berry Delicious Butter

MAKES ABOUT 2 CUPS

1 cup confectioners' sugar
¼ teaspoon fine sea salt
2 cups (4 sticks) unsalted
  butter, softened

1 teaspoon vanilla extract
½ teaspoon almond extract
2 cups fresh blackberries
  or raspberries

Combine the sugar, salt, butter, vanilla, and almond extracts in a stand mixer and beat together on low speed. Once the ingredients are combined, scrape down the bowl, and add the berries. Mix on medium speed until the butter comes together again. Transfer, either to a ramekin to serve, or wrap the berry butter in parchment paper and form into a log. Refrigerate for a few hours to develop the flavors. Store in the refrigerator for up to 1 week.

Quick Sweet Jams

IN THE COLD AND DARK of winter, my grandmother would make magic. She would sit us children at the breakfast table in front of the fire to keep warm, then she would give us presents.

The presents? A row of her homemade jams would appear in front of us, all topped with fabric and tied with kitchen twine. They were ours to open. A celebration of red and blue and orange alongside her hot-from-the-oven homemade corn muffins.

My grandmother canned her jams the traditional way and stored them in the basement on long wooden shelves. I used to help her prepare them and it would take us quite a while to work with the fruit and sterilize the jars.

Today, I love making quick jams for instant gratification depending on what I find in the farmers' market. Quick jams, for me, mean the same thing as refrigerator jams. They take no time to make, and if you have any left over they last in the refrigerator for another week or so.

It's speedy work, especially if you invest in an instant-read or candy thermometer. All you have to do is hit 220 degrees F and your jam is done!

The most rewarding part for me is that I can make jams I can't find in the store. My Apple Pie in a Jam (page 100) is like eating the filling of an apple pie, and I can have it spread on my toast in the morning. My comforting Banana Jam (page 105) is one of the most delicious jams I make and it has the added benefit of filling my kitchen with a fabulous aroma while I am cooking it. And the Grand Marnier Orange Jam (page 104) keeps the oranges as fresh and juicy as possible in a jam for an amazing wake-me-up breakfast treat.

Food Processor Blackberry Jam

MAKES 3 CUPS

6 cups fresh blackberries,
   washed and dried
5 ½ cups granulated sugar, divided

Juice of 1 ½ lemons
¼ teaspoon vanilla extract

Combine the blackberries and 1 cup sugar in a food processor and process for 25 seconds.

Transfer the blackberry mixture into a large saucepan or Dutch oven. Add the rest of the ingredients, stir, and bring to a boil over medium heat. Lower the heat to maintain a slow boil and cook, stirring often, for about 25 minutes, or until it reaches 220 degrees F on an instant-read or candy thermometer. Cool to room temperature.

Serve or transfer to glass jars with a screw top and refrigerate.

Apple Pie in a Jam

MAKES 2 CUPS

Zest and juice of 1 organic lemon,
   reserve the lemon hull
6 large mixed apples, such as
   Golden Delicious, Granny Smith,
   and Honeycrisp apples
1 tablespoon apple cider vinegar

1 tablespoon ground cinnamon
½ teaspoon ground nutmeg
¼ teaspoon ground cloves
2 ⅓ cups granulated sugar
3 tablespoons water
1 teaspoon vanilla extract

Combine the lemon zest, lemon juice, and lemon hull into a Dutch oven or heavy saucepan. Peel, core, dice the apples, tossing them in the lemon juice in the pan and stir to coat.

Add the vinegar, cinnamon, nutmeg, cloves, sugar, water, and vanilla, stir, and bring to a boil over medium heat. Reduce the heat to maintain a strong simmer and cook, stirring frequently, for 20 to 25 minutes, until it reaches 220 degrees F on an instant-read or candy thermometer, or when the jam slowly drips from a spoon.

If you wish, you can use a fork or potato masher to soften up some of the apple chunks. Stir over the heat for another 30 seconds. Remove the lemon hull and discard or keep for a snack; it tastes like candy! Sometimes I just chop it up and add it to the top of each jar.

Allow to cool to room temperature.

Transfer to glass jars with a screw top and refrigerate overnight before serving.

Blueberry Jam

MAKES 2 CUPS

4 cups fresh blueberries,
   rinsed
3 tablespoons fresh
   lemon juice
1 ½ cups granulated sugar

Combine all the ingredients
in a saucepan and bring
to a boil, stirring frequently,
over medium heat. Reduce the heat
to maintain a gentle bubble. Mash the berries
some with a potato masher or the back of a fork if
you wish, and cook, stirring frequently, for 10 minutes, or
until it is 220 degrees F on an instant-read or candy thermometer.
Let cool to room temperature.

Serve or transfer to glass jars with a screw top and refrigerate.

Fresh Strawberry Jam

MAKES 2 CUPS

4 cups roughly chopped washed
 and dried strawberries
¼ cup granulated sugar

¼ cup light brown sugar
⅛ teaspoon fine sea salt
Juice of ½ lemon

Combine all the ingredients in a large skillet or saucepan and bring to a simmer over medium heat. Mash the strawberries with a potato masher to the consistency you desire and continue to cook at a low boil until it thickens and the spoon leaves a dry trail when dragged across the bottom of the skillet or it reaches 220 degrees F on an instant-read or candy thermometer. Allow to cool to room temperature.

Serve or transfer to a glass jar with a screw top and refrigerate.

Fresh Strawberry-Raspberry Jam

MAKES 2 CUPS

16 ounces fresh strawberries,
 washed, hulled, and sliced
8 ounces fresh raspberries, rinsed

¾ cup granulated sugar
Juice of ½ lemon
1 teaspoon vanilla extract

Combine the strawberries, raspberries, sugar, lemon juice, and vanilla in a large pot over medium heat. Cook, stirring frequently, for 10 to 12 minutes, or until the mixture reaches 220 degrees F on an instant-read or candy thermometer. You will start to see bubbles forming on the top and when you see no more bubbles, the jam should be done. Let cool to room temperature.

Serve or transfer to glass jars with a screw top and refrigerate.

No-Cook Purple Grape and Chia Seed Jam

MAKES 2 CUPS

4 tablespoons chia seeds
2 cups seedless purple grapes
2 to 3 tablespoons honey or maple syrup

Process the chia seeds in a coffee or spice grinder until it is a powder.

Pulse the grapes in a food processor until they are broken down and liquefied. Add 2 tablespoons of honey and the chia powder and process until combined. Taste and add the remaining 1 tablespoon honey, if desired.

Transfer to glass jars with a screw top and refrigerate overnight before serving.

Autumn Pumpkin Butter

MAKES 1¾ CUPS

1 (15-ounce) can pumpkin purée
¼ cup packed light brown sugar
1 teaspoon ground cinnamon
1 teaspoon pumpkin pie spice (optional)
1½ tablespoons honey
⅛ teaspoon fine sea salt

Combine all the ingredients in a saucepan and cook over medium heat, stirring frequently, for about 10 minutes, or until it has turned a darker color and is thicker. Cool to room temperature.

Serve or transfer to glass jars with a screw top and refrigerate.

Southern Jezebel Sauce

MAKES 1 CUP

1 (5-ounce) jar apple jelly
1 (5-ounce) jar pineapple preserves
1 ½ teaspoons Dijon mustard
⅓ cup prepared horseradish
½ teaspoon ground cinnamon
¼ teaspoon crushed red pepper flakes

Briskly stir all the ingredients together in a bowl.

Transfer to a serving bowl or a glass jar with a screw top and refrigerate. This is popular over cream cheese and crackers and would go well on a cheese or charcuterie board.

Grand Marnier Orange Jam

MAKES 1 CUP

5 organic oranges, such as naval, mandarin, cara cara, or blood orange

1 organic lemon
1 cup granulated sugar
2 tablespoons Grand Marnier

Zest 1 orange and transfer the zest to a Dutch oven or large pot. Cut that orange into small dice and toss into the pot. Peel the remaining 4 oranges, remove as much of the white pith as you can, then cut the flesh into small dice. Transfer to the pot. Discard the peels.

Cut the lemon in half. Finely chop one half and toss into the Dutch oven. Squeeze the juice from the other half into the pot and discard the hull.

Add the sugar, stir well, and let sit for 45 minutes. At this point, you can mash down the fruit with a potato masher or fork if you wish to get more juice out of the oranges.

Cook, stirring frequently, over medium heat until it has thickened and reached 220 degrees F on an instant-read or candy thermometer. Take the pan off the heat and stir in the Grand Marnier. Cool to room temperature.

Serve or transfer to glass jars with a screw top and refrigerate.

Banana Jam

MAKES 5 TO 6 CUPS

5 cups thickly sliced very ripe
bananas (about 5 bananas)
Juice of 1 lemon
¾ cup water
½ cup granulated sugar
½ cup packed light brown sugar
1 tablespoon honey

¼ teaspoon fine sea salt
1 teaspoon ground cinnamon
⅛ teaspoon ground nutmeg
1 teaspoon vanilla extract
½ teaspoon ground
cardamom (optional)
1 tablespoon dark rum (optional)

Combine the bananas and lemon juice in a bowl and toss to coat.

Combine the water and sugars in a saucepan and cook over medium until the sugar is dissolved. Whisk in the honey, salt, cinnamon, nutmeg, and vanilla. Stir in the bananas and bring to a boil. Lower the heat to maintain a low rolling boil and cook, stirring occasionally, for 30 to 35 minutes or until it turns a thick golden brown and the mixture reaches 220 degrees F on an instant-read or candy thermometer. Mix in the cardamom and rum, if using. Let cool to room temperature.

Serve or transfer to glass jars with a screw top and refrigerate.

Quick Savory Jams

WHEN I LEARNED how to make savory jams it was a revelation. They were so delicious and interesting that it compelled me to experiment with different flavors. My favorite so far is my mouthwatering Fig and Ruby Port Jam (page 109). In the summer when there is an abundance of tomatoes, I make tons of my Balsamic Cherry Tomato Jam (page 108). I eat it by the spoonful. And when I make a roast I always make my Candied Olive Jam (page 108) for a condiment.

Candied Olive Jam

MAKES 1 CUP

1 ½ cup canned pitted black olives, drained and coarsely chopped
½ (7-ounce) jar oil-cured pitted black olives, coarsely chopped

½ cup granulated sugar
Extra-virgin olive oil, if needed

Combine the olives and sugar in a saucepan and bring to a boil over medium to medium-high heat. Let it bubble away for 4 to 5 minutes, or until the liquid is reduced, the sugar is dissolved, and it has a smooth consistency. Add a few drops of olive oil to thin out, if desired, and stir vigorously until smooth. Let cool to room temperature.

Serve or transfer to glass jars with a screw top and refrigerate. Let come to room temperature before serving.

Balsamic Cherry Tomato Jam

MAKES 2 CUPS

2 tablespoons extra-virgin olive oil
⅔ cup finely chopped white onion
1 pint ripe cherry or grape tomatoes, halved
¼ cup honey
½ teaspoon ground cinnamon

½ cup packed light brown sugar
½ teaspoon fine sea salt
½ teaspoon crushed red pepper flakes
½ teaspoon fine sea salt
3 tablespoons dark balsamic vinegar

Heat the olive oil in a large saucepan over medium-high heat. Add the onion and cook, stirring often, for 5 minutes.

Add the rest of the ingredients, mix well, and bring to a boil. Reduce the heat to maintain a simmer and cook, stirring often, for 20 minutes.

Use the back of a slotted spoon or a potato masher and mash down the tomatoes a bit and flatten most of them. Continue to simmer for another 25 minutes, or until the jam thickens. Allow to cool to room temperature.

Serve or transfer to glass jars with a screw top and refrigerate for up to 2 weeks.

Fig and Ruby Port Jam

MAKES 2 CUPS

8 ounces dried figs, stems removed and cut in quarters
¾ cup granulated sugar
3 tablespoons freshly squeezed lemon juice
1 teaspoon lemon zest

1 cup ruby port wine, plus more if needed
1 sprig fresh rosemary, leaves only, minced
½ teaspoon fine sea salt, plus more if needed

Combine all the ingredients in a large saucepan or Dutch oven and bring to a boil over medium heat. Reduce the heat to maintain a gentle simmer and cook for 7 minutes.

Transfer the mixture to a blender or food processor and pulse until the jam still has bits of figs noticeable.

Return the mixture to the saucepan and cook until thickened and a spatula swiped over the bottom of the pan leaves a trail. The jam will thicken as it cools. Taste and add salt or more port wine. Allow to cool to room temperature.

Serve or transfer to glass jars with a screw top and refrigerate for up to 2 weeks.

Caramelized Onion Jam

MAKES 2 CUPS

1 medium white onion
2 medium yellow onions
3 tablespoons extra-virgin olive oil
4 tablespoons granulated sugar
4 tablespoons light brown sugar

1 tablespoon coarsely chopped
   fresh rosemary
1/2 teaspoon fine sea salt
1/2 to 3/4 cup white balsamic vinegar

Thinly slice the onions, then cut them into half-moons.

Heat the oil in a large saucepan or skillet over medium heat. Toss the onions into the skillet and cook, stirring frequently, for 15 minutes, or until they are beginning to turn golden brown.

Add the granulated sugar and continue to cook until the onions are caramelized, 5 to 7 minutes. Stir in the brown sugar, rosemary, salt, and 1/2 cup of vinegar. Taste and add up to 1/4 cup more vinegar, if desired. Reduce the heat to medium-low and cook, stirring frequently, for up to 1 hour, or until the jam is thick. Allow to cool to room temperature.

Serve or transfer to glass jars with a screw top and refrigerate for up to 1 week.

Apricot-Onion Jam

MAKES 1 1/2 CUPS

3 tablespoons unsalted butter
1 cup chopped yellow onion
1/2 cup chopped red onion
1/2 cup finely chopped dried apricots

1/4 cup granulated sugar
1/4 cup packed light brown sugar
1 tablespoon white balsamic vinegar
1/4 teaspoon salt

Melt the butter in a large saucepan or Dutch oven over medium heat. Add the onions and cook for 4 minutes. Add the rest of the ingredients and continue cooking, stirring frequently, for about 20 minutes, or until the jam is thickened and when you swipe a spatula across the bottom of the pan the jam leaves a trail. Cool to room temperature.

Serve or transfer to glass jars with a screw top and refrigerate for up to 2 weeks.

Sweet and Salty Pineapple-Bacon Jam

MAKES 1 CUP

1 pound bacon, finely chopped
1 small yellow onion, cut
    into small dice
3 large garlic cloves, finely chopped
½ cup packed light brown sugar
1 tablespoon honey

1 tablespoon distilled white vinegar
2 teaspoons Dijon mustard
⅛ teaspoon ground cloves
⅓ cup canned crushed pineapple,
    with the juice

In a large skillet over medium-high heat, cook the bacon until brown. Drain on paper towels and set aside.

Remove all but 2 tablespoons of the bacon grease from the skillet. Add the onion and garlic and cook over medium heat for about 5 minutes, or until the onion is softened.

Add the brown sugar, honey, vinegar, Dijon mustard, and cloves and cook, stirring frequently, until the sugar melts. Add the crushed pineapple and stir well. Add the reserved bacon and bring to a boil. Reduce the heat to a simmer and cook, stirring frequently, for about 60 minutes, or until the jam thickens. Cool to room temperature.

Serve or transfer to glass jars with a screw top and refrigerate for up to 2 months.

Chutneys

CHUTNEY IS A LOT LIKE a savory jam but not always as sweet, and is made with vinegar as well as with sugar. Traditionally an accompaniment for Indian recipes or roast meats, you can also mix it into mayonnaise for much more interesting sandwiches, drape it over cream cheese or a hunk of cheese and serve with a sliced baguette, spoon it onto a burger, and even whip it into sour cream or softened goat cheese or ricotta for a quick dip.

Many cultures make their own forms of chutney. I like making Italian mostarda to serve with cheeses or on a charcuterie board. And in New England they make a great cranberry chutney usually served around Thanksgiving. So give the following chutney recipes a go!

Major Grey's Chutney

MAKES 2 CUPS

1 pound fresh mangoes, peeled,
   pitted, cut into small dice
1 medium yellow or Vidalia
   onion, finely chopped
¼ cup minced or grated fresh ginger
½ cup golden raisins
¼ cup distilled white vinegar
   or apple cider vinegar

¼ teaspoon fine sea salt
1 ½ cups granulated sugar (brown
   sugar will turn it brown)
1 garlic clove, finely chopped
½ teaspoon ground cinnamon
¼ teaspoon ground cloves
¼ cup store-bought ginger
   jam or preserves

Combine all the ingredients, except the ginger jam, in a saucepan, whisk to combine, and bring to a boil over medium-high heat. Reduce the heat to maintain a simmer and cook for 35 to 50 minutes, stirring frequently, until thickened. Stir in the ginger jam until well combined. Allow to cool to room temperature.

Serve or transfer to glass jars with a screw top and refrigerate for up to 1 month.

Fresh Mint and Cilantro Chutney

MAKES 1½ CUPS

1 bunch fresh cilantro
1 cup tightly packed
   fresh mint leaves
½ jalapeño pepper or 2 Thai
   chiles, stemmed and sliced
2 garlic cloves, sliced
½ teaspoon fine sea salt
½ teaspoon ground cumin

2 tablespoons freshly squeezed
   lemon or lime juice, plus
   more as needed
½ cup full-fat yogurt
½ teaspoon honey
1 tablespoon neutral oil
1 tablespoon distilled white vinegar

Cut off about 2 inches of the cilantro stems, discard, then toss the rest into a blender. Add the rest of the ingredients and process until smooth. If needed, add 1 tablespoon of water or 1 more tablespoon of lemon or lime juice to the blender as you process. You might need to stop and stir a couple of times. Serve or transfer to glass jars with a screw top and refrigerate for up to 2 days or transfer to an ice cube tray and freeze for up to 1 month.

New England Cranberry Chutney

MAKES 2½ CUPS

1 tablespoon neutral oil
1 (1-inch) knob peeled ginger, grated on large holes of a box grater
½ cup red onion or 1 shallot, finely chopped
¾ cups granulated sugar
¼ cup honey or maple syrup

½ cup cranberry juice or orange juice
3 tablespoons distilled white vinegar
2 teaspoons Dijon mustard
½ teaspoon fine sea salt
1 (12-ounce) bag fresh cranberries
½ cup dried cranberries
2 tablespoons orange marmalade

Heat the oil in a large saucepan or Dutch oven over medium heat. Add the ginger and onion and cook for 3 minutes, stirring frequently.

Add the sugar, honey, juice, vinegar, mustard, and salt and bring to a boil. Toss in the fresh and dried cranberries and return to a boil. Reduce the heat to maintain a low boil and cook for 10 to 12 minutes, stirring frequently, until the cranberries have popped and are soft enough to mash. Use a potato masher or fork to flatten some of them if you wish. Taste and add more sugar if desired.

Stir in the marmalade and take the pan off the heat. Cover and allow to cool to room temperature. It will thicken as it cools.

Serve or transfer to glass jars with a screw top and refrigerate for up to 2 weeks.

Fresh Peach Chutney

MAKES 2 CUPS

2 tablespoons extra-virgin olive oil
½ small red onion, finely diced
3 teaspoons minced fresh ginger
1 small jalapeño pepper,
    seeded, and finely diced
4 fresh, firm peaches, pitted,
    peeled, and cut into small dice
1 tablespoon distilled white vinegar

2 tablespoons apple cider vinegar
3 tablespoons light brown sugar
½ teaspoon fine sea salt
¼ teaspoon ground cinnamon
¼ teaspoon ground nutmeg
1 teaspoon Dijon mustard
¼ cup minced fresh cilantro leaves

Heat the oil in a saucepan over medium heat. Add the onion, ginger, and jalapeño and cook, stirring often, for 3 minutes, or until the onion has softened and is translucent.

Add the peaches and cook for 3 minutes. Add the vinegars, brown sugar, salt, cinnamon, nutmeg, and mustard and bring to a boil. Reduce the heat to maintain a rolling simmer and cook for 10 to 15 minutes, or until the sauce thickens. Take the pan off the heat and stir in the cilantro leaves. Let cool to room temperature.

Fresh Rhubarb Chutney

MAKES 2 CUPS

2 cups ½-inch slices fresh rhubarb
½ cup granulated sugar
¼ cup honey
1 tablespoon distilled white vinegar
2 tablespoons apple cider vinegar

1 medium shallot, finely diced
1 teaspoon vanilla extract
½ cup fresh cranberries
½ teaspoon ground allspice
⅛ teaspoon ground cloves

Combine all the ingredients into a large saucepan over medium heat and bring to a simmer. Cook, stirring frequently, for 15 to 20 minutes, or until the mixture thickens. Allow to cool to room temperature.

Serve or transfer to glass jars with a screw top and refrigerate for 2 days before serving. It can be refrigerated for up to 2 days.

Tropical Pineapple and Mango Chutney

MAKES 3 CUPS

1 cup diced fresh pineapple (canned in a pinch), plus juice
3 large underripe mangoes, pitted, peeled, and cut into small dice, reserving the juice
½ cup distilled white vinegar
2 tablespoons extra-virgin olive oil
1 small red onion, diced
1 (2-inch) knob peeled ginger, diced
¼ teaspoon crushed red pepper flakes

3 large garlic cloves, diced
2 tablespoons light brown sugar
2 tablespoons curry powder
1 teaspoon ground cumin
1 teaspoon ground allspice
½ teaspoon fine sea salt
¼ cup golden raisins
¼ cup minced fresh mint leaves

Combine the pineapple, its juice, and the mango with its juice in a large bowl. Add the vinegar and stir to combine.

Heat the olive oil in a large saucepan over medium heat. Add the onion, ginger, red pepper flakes, and garlic and cook, stirring frequently, for 5 to 7 minutes, or until the onion has softened and is translucent.

Add the brown sugar, curry powder, cumin, allspice, salt, and raisins and cook, stirring well, for 3 minutes.

Add the fruit and bring to a rolling simmer, stirring frequently. You want to cook down the liquid and have the fruit become soft and take on a glossy appearance. Take the pan off the heat, stir in the minced mint, and cool to room temperature.

Serve or transfer to glass jars with a screw top and refrigerate for up to 2 weeks.

Northern Italian Apricot and Cherry Mostarda

MAKES 3 CUPS

1 tablespoon extra-virgin olive oil
1 large shallot, minced
1 pound Granny Smith
   apples, with peel
1 pound Bosc pears, with peel
Juice of 1 lemon
¾ cup granulated sugar
2 tablespoons light brown sugar
½ teaspoon fine sea salt
3 teaspoons Dijon mustard

1 tablespoon yellow mustard seeds
6 ounces dried cherries,
   coarsely chopped
½ cup dried apricots,
   cut into quarters
3 cups dry white wine
½ cup distilled white vinegar
   or apple cider vinegar
½ cup maraschino cherries,
   sliced in half

Heat the oil in a large saucepan or Dutch oven over medium heat. Toss in the shallot, and cook for about 5 minutes, until it is softened.

Cut the apples and pears into ½-inch pieces. Toss them in a bowl, pour over the lemon juice, and stir to thoroughly coat them. Toss the apples and pears into the saucepan.

Add the sugars, salt, mustard, mustard seeds, dried cherries, dried apricots, wine, and vinegar, stir well, and bring to a boil over medium-high heat. Reduce the heat to maintain a low boil and let the mixture bubble for about 1 hour, or until it becomes syrupy and thick. Stir in the maraschino cherries. Allow to cool to room temperature.

Serve or transfer to glass jars with a screw top and refrigerate for up to
3 weeks.

Kumquat Chutney

MAKES 2 CUPS

2 tablespoons extra-virgin olive oil
1 medium shallot, finely chopped
1 teaspoon fine sea salt
1 garlic clove, finely chopped
1 (1-inch) knob peeled ginger, grated
   on large holes of a box grater
2 tablespoons granulated sugar
3 tablespoons light brown sugar
1 teaspoon curry powder
½ teaspoon ground cumin

1 teaspoon ground cinnamon
¼ teaspoon ground cloves
1 whole star anise
¼ teaspoon crushed red
   pepper flakes
18 kumquats, sliced then coarsely
   chopped and seeds removed
2 tablespoons distilled white vinegar
½ cup orange juice

Heat the olive oil in a large saucepan over medium heat. Add the shallot and
cook, stirring frequently, for 4 minutes. Add the salt, garlic, and ginger and
cook for 5 minutes. Add the sugars, curry powder, cumin, cinnamon, cloves,
star anise, and red pepper flakes, stir, and cook for 2 minutes.

Add the kumquats and bring to a boil over medium-high heat. Reduce the
heat to maintain a low boil and let it bubble for 10 to 15 minutes, or until the
kumquats are soft and the liquid has thickened. Remove the star anise and
discard. Allow the chutney to cool to room temperature.

Serve or transfer to glass jars with a screw top and refrigerate for up to
2 weeks.

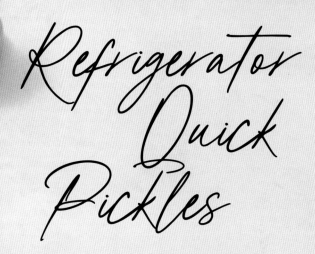

Refrigerator Quick Pickles

QUICK AND EASY, homemade pickles are one of the most requested recipes from my friends when I serve them, probably because they are so vibrant in flavor and color and crunch compared to store-bought. You can really spice them up by adding anything you can think of to them. And they take only minutes to make.

The first recipe is a basic one that you can use for any vegetables you have on hand. If you have a cucumber, maybe a red bell pepper, some cauliflower florets, maybe some dill fronds, a few leftover asparagus spears, throw them into the jar. You can also choose to use just one vegetable. They will be ready to enjoy after 24 hours in the refrigerator.

The same thing can be done with fruits you may have on hand. Try throwing in a sliced peach, some blueberries, grapes, melon, or any variety of fruits as they are all delicious pickled. Try my recipe for Fall Pickled Apples (page 130) or Pickled Red Grapes (page 131)!

For topping burgers, I love my Delicious Candied Pickled Jalapeños, a pile of my Pickled Red Onions (page 125) or my crunchy Basic Sweet Bread and Butter Pickles (page 123). Once you make your own, you won't look back.

Easy Vegetable or Fruit Homemade Pickles

MAKES 1 QUART

1 cup water
2 cups distilled white vinegar
  or apple cider vinegar
2 tablespoons McCormick
  pickling spice
1 red onion, thinly sliced
2 cups granulated sugar
1 tablespoon sea salt

Jars packed with your choice
  of vegetables and/or fruit
Your choice of fresh herbs, such
  as dill, rosemary, thyme,
  oregano, basil, cilantro
Your choice of spices, such
  as red pepper flakes

Combine the water, vinegar, pickling spice, onion, sugar, and salt in a sauce-pan and bring to a boil. Reduce the heat to maintain a simmer for 2 minutes. Pour the mixture into the jar(s) to completely cover the vegetables and/or fruit. Let cool to room temperature and then screw on the top.

Refrigerate for 24 hours before eating. They can be stored in the refrigerator for up to 2 months.

Quick Dill Pickles

MAKES 1 QUART

4 fresh dill fronds, coarsely chopped
4 large garlic cloves, 2
  smashed, 2 sliced
2 bay leaves
5 Kirby, pickling, or mini
  Persian cucumbers
½ teaspoon yellow mustard seeds

1 teaspoon black peppercorns
1 tablespoon fine sea salt
⅛ teaspoon crushed red
  pepper flakes
1⅓ cups water
⅔ cup distilled white vinegar
1 teaspoon sugar

Combine the dill, garlic, and bay leaves in the bottom of a wide-mouth 1-quart glass jar with a screw top.

Trim the ends off the cucumbers, and then cut them into 4 long spears. Alternatively, cut them into ¼-inch coins. Add the cucumbers to the jar.

Combine the mustard seeds, peppercorns, salt, pepper flakes, water, vinegar, and sugar in a saucepan and cook over medium-high heat until the sugar is dissolved. Pour the mixture over the cucumbers in the jar to cover. Allow to come to room temperature and then screw on the top.

Refrigerate for 24 hours before eating. They can be stored in the refrigerator for up to 2 months.

Basic Sweet
Bread and Butter Pickles

MAKES 3 PINTS

7 to 8 pickling, Kirby, or Persian pickles (regular cucumbers may come out mushy)
1 ¼ cups granulated sugar
1 cup apple cider vinegar

½ cup distilled white vinegar
1 tablespoon McCormick pickling spices
1 teaspoon yellow mustard seeds
¼ cup honey (optional)

Cut the pickles with a crinkle cutter or sharp knife into ¼-inch slices. Pack the cucumbers into glass jars with screw tops.

To make the brine, combine the rest of the ingredients, including the honey, if using, into a saucepan over medium-high heat and bring to a boil. Reduce the heat to a simmer and cook, stirring frequently, until the sugar has dissolved. Pour the mixture over the pickles in the jars all the way to the top and let cool to room temperature.

Screw on the top and refrigerate for at least 24 hours before eating. They can be stored in the refrigerator for up to 2 months.

Honey-Mustard Bread and Butter Pickles

MAKES 3 PINTS

After making the brine for the Basic Sweet Bread and Butter Pickles recipe (page 123), use a fork to mix 2 teaspoons honey with 2 teaspoons Dijon mustard then mix into the brine. Taste and add more of each to your taste. Pour this brine over the pickles in the jar.

Delicious Candied Pickled Jalapeños

MAKES 1 PINT

1 pound fresh jalapeños
3 fresh red Fresno hot peppers
½ cup apple cider vinegar
½ cup distilled white vinegar
1 cup granulated sugar

½ cup light brown sugar
1 heaping tablespoon
    McCormick pickling spice
⅛ teaspoon fine sea salt

Wearing rubber or disposable gloves, cut the jalapeños in coins, keeping the seeds. Toss them into a bowl. Cut the red Fresno chiles in half vertically and slice them thinly. Throw them into the bowl.

Combine the vinegars, sugars, pickling spice, and salt in a saucepan over medium-high heat. Cook, stirring until dissolved, about 4 minutes.

Add the peppers, mix well to coat, and bring to a boil. Reduce the heat to maintain a simmer and cook 5 minutes. Using a slotted spoon, transfer the jalapeños into a clean pint jar.

Bring the liquid back to a boil over high heat. Reduce the heat to medium-high and cook at a low boil until reduced by half, about 8 minutes. Pour the mixture over the peppers in the jar and let cool to room temperature.

Screw on the top and refrigerate for at least 24 hours before eating. You can store them in the refrigerator for up to 2 months, if they last that long.

Pickled Red Onions

MAKES 3 HALF-PINT JARS

2 red onions, thinly sliced
   into half moons
3 bay leaves
3 tablespoons chopped fresh
   dill fronds or fresh thyme
   leaves, divided (optional)
½ cup distilled white vinegar
   or apple cider vinegar

½ cup water
3 garlic cloves, smashed
2 tablespoons granulated sugar
1 tablespoon honey or hot honey
½ teaspoon fine sea salt
1 teaspoon peppercorns
1 cinnamon stick

Separate the sliced onions with your fingers and stuff all of them into the glass jars with screw tops, filling them all the way to the top. Add 1 bay leaf and 1 tablespoon dill, if using, to each jar.

To make the brine, combine the vinegar, water, garlic, sugar, honey, salt, peppercorns, and cinnamon stick in a saucepan and bring to a boil over medium-high heat. Reduce the heat to maintain a simmer and whisk for about 1 minutes, or until the sugar is dissolved. Pour the brine over the onions all the way to the top and allow to cool to room temperature.

Screw on the tops and refrigerate for 24 hours before using. They can be stored in the refrigerator for up to 2 weeks.

Springtime Pickled Asparagus

MAKES 1 QUART

2 fresh dill fronds
2 garlic cloves, sliced
2 teaspoons McCormick
    pickling spice
1 pound asparagus,
    cleaned and dried

1 cup water
1 cup distilled white vinegar
2 teaspoons fine sea salt
3 tablespoons granulated sugar

Put the dill fronds, garlic, and pickling spice into the bottom of a wide-mouth 1-quart glass jar with a screw top.

Snap off enough of the ends of each asparagus spear so that they fit nicely into the jar and arrange them tip side up.

Combine the water, vinegar, salt, and sugar in a saucepan and bring to a boil. Cook, stirring, until the sugar is dissolved. Pour the mixture over the asparagus spears. Allow to cool to room temperature.

Screw on the top and refrigerate overnight before eating. They can be stored in the refrigerator for up to 2 weeks.

Pickled Ginger with Pink Peppercorns

MAKES 1 HALF-PINT JAR

1 (2-inch) knob ginger, peeled
1¾ cup distilled white vinegar
½ cup granulated sugar
⅛ teaspoon fine sea salt

⅛ teaspoon ground cinnamon
1 tablespoon pink peppercorns,
    freshly ground or pounded
    with a rolling pin

With a vegetable peeler, peel the ginger into thin slices.

Combine the vinegar and sugar in a medium saucepan over medium heat and cook until the sugar is dissolved. Add the salt, cinnamon, and ground pink peppercorns. Add the sliced ginger and let cool for about 4 minutes.

Transfer the mixture to a glass jar, screw on the top, and refrigerate for at least 24 hours before eating. They can be stored in the refrigerator for up to 1 month.

Transfer the beets to a colander in the sink and, wearing rubber gloves to keep your hands from staining, peel the beets. Cut them into coins or chunks.

Combine the rest of the ingredients in a saucepan and bring to a boil over medium-high heat. Put the sliced beets into glass pint jars. Pour the hot brine over them to cover and screw on the tops. Let cool to room temperature.

Refrigerate for 3 days before eating. They can be stored for up to 4 days.

Pickled Beets

MAKES 1 QUART PLUS 1 PINT

2 pounds beets
1 cup apple cider vinegar
½ cup rice wine vinegar, white wine vinegar, or red wine vinegar
1 cup water

1 teaspoon fine sea salt
1 teaspoon ground cloves
1 teaspoon ground cinnamon
1 ¼ cups granulated sugar

Remove the stems and leaves from the beets and save them for sautéing in olive oil another day. Put the beets, skin on, into a saucepan, cover with water, and cook on medium-high heat until very tender. The cooking time depends on the size of the beets.

Pickled Red Cabbage

MAKES 1 QUART

2 pounds red cabbage
1 ¼ cups water
1 cup apple cider vinegar
¼ cup dry white wine
2 garlic cloves, minced
1 teaspoon fine sea salt

1 tablespoon granulated sugar
1 tablespoon honey
¼ teaspoon allspice
5 black peppercorns
4 juniper berries (optional)

Cut the cabbage into large chunks and shred on the shredding blade of a food processor or slice very thinly with a knife. Alternatively, you can finely chop it. Pack the cabbage into glass jars with screw tops.

Combine the rest of the ingredients in a saucepan and bring to a boil over medium-high heat, whisking until the sugar is dissolved. Pour the brine over the cabbage in the jars until the cabbage is totally covered. Screw on the tops and allow to come to room temperature.

Refrigerate for 2 days before using. They can be refrigerated for up to 2 weeks.

Pickled Button Mushrooms

MAKES 1 QUART

1 pound fresh small button
    mushrooms, cleaned
1 bay leaf
1 teaspoon whole black peppercorns
½ teaspoon yellow mustard seeds
2 large garlic cloves, minced
¼ teaspoon crushed red
    pepper flakes
1 sprig fresh thyme, leaves only

½ teaspoon Italian seasoning
1 ¼ cup red wine vinegar
¾ cup water
2 teaspoons granulated sugar
1 teaspoon fine sea salt
¼ cup extra-virgin olive oil
¼ cup minced Italian flat-
    leaf parsley leaves

Combine the mushrooms, bay leaf, peppercorns, mustard seeds, garlic, red pepper flakes, thyme, Italian seasoning, vinegar, water, sugar, and salt in a saucepan and bring to a boil over medium-high heat. Reduce the heat to maintain a simmer and stir for about 4 minutes, or until the sugar is dissolved.

Transfer everything to glass jars with screw tops, making sure to top off each jar with enough brine to cover the mushrooms. Screw on the top and allow to come to room temperature.

Refrigerate for 2 days before eating. When you are ready to serve, transfer the pickled mushrooms to a bowl, drizzle them with the olive oil, toss in the minced parsley, and mix to coat.

Pickled Avocados

MAKES 1 QUART

1 cup water
1 cup distilled white vinegar, rice
    vinegar, or white balsamic vinegar
1 tablespoon fine sea salt
1/3 cup granulated sugar
3 garlic cloves, sliced
1 organic lime, halved

1/2 organic lime, juiced
3 to 4 large slightly unripe
    avocados, pitted, peeled, thickly
    sliced or cut into chunks
1 to 2 bay leaves
1/4 cup chopped fresh cilantro leaves

To make the brine, combine the water, vinegar, salt, and sugar in a saucepan over medium heat and whisk until the sugar has dissolved. Add the garlic, lime halves, and lime juice, stir, and take the pan off the heat.

Layer the avocado slices in a quart-size glass jar with a screw top and add the lime slices. Slip in 1 or 2 bay leaves and the cilantro leaves. Pour the brine over the top to cover the avocado. Screw on the top, shake a bit to mix, and refrigerate for at least 5 hours before eating.

They can be stored in the refrigerator for up to 2 weeks.

Fall Pickled Apples

MAKES 2 PINTS

1 cup apple cider vinegar
1 cup water
2 tablespoons McCormick
   pickling spice
2 cinnamon sticks, broken in half
1 teaspoon fine sea salt

6 tablespoons honey
2 tablespoons light brown sugar
1 tablespoon granulated sugar
3 to 4 Golden Delicious apples,
   washed, dried, and cut into
   ¼-inch-thick slices

Into a medium saucepan, combine the vinegar, water, pickling spice, cinnamon sticks, salt, honey, and sugars and bring to a boil over medium-high heat. Reduce the heat to maintain a simmer and stir until the sugar has dissolved. Take the pan off the heat.

Distribute the apples evenly between 2 pint-size glass jars with screw tops. Top the apples equally with the brine in the saucepan. Screw on the tops and let cool to room temperature.

Refrigerate for at least 24 hours before eating. They are best the next day or the day after to preserve the crunch of the apples.

Pickled Pineapple and Maraschino Cherries

MAKES 1 QUART

1 fresh ripe pineapple or 1 (20-ounce)
   can pineapple chunks
1 (8-ounce) jar maraschino cherries
2 cups distilled white vinegar
1 cup water

1¼ cup granulated sugar
6 whole cloves
1 cinnamon stick, broken in two
2 teaspoons fine sea salt

Peel and core the pineapple, cut into rounds, then cut into quarters or small chunks and place them in a large saucepan. Set aside.

Combine 2 tablespoons of liquid from the maraschino cherries, the vinegar, water, sugar, cloves, cinnamon stick, and salt in a saucepan, stir, and bring to a boil over medium-high heat. Reduce the heat to maintain a simmer and cook for 4 minutes.

Use a slotted spoon or tongs to transfer the pineapple chunks to a wide-mouth 1-quart glass jar with a screw top. Layer in some maraschino cherries and the cloves and cinnamon stick as you add the pineapple chunks. When you have filled the jar, cover the pineapple with the brine. Screw on the top and let cool to room temperature.

Refrigerate for 2 days before serving. They can be stored in the refrigerator for up to 2 weeks.

Pickled Red Grapes

MAKES 1 PINT

2 cinnamon sticks
1 pound small seedless red grapes
1 ½ cup distilled white vinegar
1 cup water
½ cup granulated sugar

3 tablespoons honey
⅛ teaspoon Chinese five-spice powder
2 teaspoons McCormick pickling spice

Put a cinnamon stick in each of 2 glass jars with a screw top or put them both in if you are using 1 jar.

Cut into the grapes halfway down, without slicing all the way, so the brine can reach the inside. Transfer the grapes to the glass jar(s).

In a small saucepan, bring the vinegar, water, sugar, honey, five-spice powder, and pickling spice to a boil over medium-high heat. Pour the mixture over the grapes to cover. Screw on the tops and let the jars cool to room temperature.

Refrigerate for at least 24 hours before eating. The grapes can be refrigerated for up to 3 days.

Relishes

I BECAME A DEVOTED FAN of relish after I was introduced to the burgers at a restaurant in New York City called Hamburger Heaven. Every table had a jar of their sweet red pepper relish, and every time I ate there, I emptied that jar onto my burger. It was so good. So addictive. It made the burger. And it was the reason I went back again and again over the years.

A good relish is memorable, not just a last-minute thought, but a star element when you bite into a burger or hot dog.

Two-Color Raw Corn Relish

MAKES 2 CUPS

3 medium ears fresh corn, both
   white and yellow, shucked
1 medium red bell pepper, seeded
   and cut into small dice
1 small green bell pepper, seeded
   and cut into small dice
1 cup Vidalia onion or red
   onion, cut into small dice

¼ jalapeño pepper, minced
   including seeds
4 tablespoons vinegar
2 tablespoons extra-virgin
   olive oil or avocado oil
1 tablespoon granulated sugar
½ teaspoon fine sea salt
1 teaspoon celery seeds
¼ teaspoon ground allspice

Cut the kernels of corn off the cobs and toss them into a bowl. Add the red
and green peppers, onion, and jalapeño and stir to mix.

In a small bowl, combine the vinegar, oil, sugar, salt, celery seeds, and allspice
and whisk well to combine. Pour the mixture into a saucepan, bring to a simmer,
and stir just long enough for the sugar to melt. Cool to room temperature.

Bit by bit, pour the vinegar mixture into the corn mixture while constantly
stirring until you use just enough to coat the corn with flavor without it
becoming too liquid.

Serve, or transfer the mixture to a glass jar with
a screw top, seal, and store in the refrigerator
for up to 2 weeks.

Sweet Gherkin Pickle Relish

MAKES 2 CUPS

2 cups store-bought sliced
   sweet pickled gherkins
12 leaves fresh Italian
   flat-leaf parsley
3 teaspoons granulated sugar

2 teaspoons distilled white vinegar
1 teaspoon ground cinnamon
¼ teaspoon ground cloves
1 teaspoon Dijon mustard

Combine the gherkins and parsley in a food processor and pulse until finely chopped. Transfer to a bowl, add the rest of the ingredients, and stir well to combine. Serve, or transfer the mixture to a glass jar with a screw top, seal, and store in the refrigerator for up to 2 weeks.

Quick Hot Dog Relish

MAKES 2 ½ CUPS

2 cups finely chopped store-bought dill pickles
2 tablespoons pickle juice from the dill pickle jar

2 tablespoons minced fresh dill
1 teaspoon onion powder
½ cup finely diced red onion
2 teaspoons Dijon mustard

Combine all the ingredients in a bowl and stir to combine. Cover and refrigerate for 2 hours before using. If you would like a finer texture, pulse the mixture in a food processor a few times. Serve, or transfer the mixture to a glass jar with a screw top, seal, and store in the refrigerator.

New England Cranberry Relish

MAKES 2 CUPS

12 ounces fresh cranberries
Zest and juice of 1 organic orange
½ cup finely chopped walnuts

½ cup granulated sugar
¼ cup packed light brown sugar

Combine all the ingredients in a food processor and pulse until finely chopped. Transfer the mixture to a saucepan over medium heat and cook for about 2 minutes, or until the sugars are dissolved. Cool to room temperature. Serve, or transfer the mixture to a glass jar with a screw top, seal, and store in the refrigerator for up to 2 weeks.

Barbecue Sauces

THIS IS ONE OF the store-bought condiments that typically is made with high-fructose corn syrup or lots of sugar and sodium. If you would rather not consume those ingredients, or reduce them, especially in the quantity they are processed with, you can make your own. It takes a bowl, a whisk, and some stuff you probably have in your pantry to make a basic sauce.

I think you will like my recipe for sticky Korean-Style Barbecue Sauce (page 145) slathered on almost anything. The recipe for my tangy sweet Alabama White Barbecue Sauce (page 147) is popular on chicken but I also love it on a burger. When peaches are in season, there's nothing like grilling with my Fresh Peach Barbecue Sauce (page 147) and then having more of it in a bowl to dip the grilled bits in again.

Basic Barbecue Sauce

MAKES 2½ CUPS

2 tablespoons extra-virgin olive oil
½ onion, finely chopped
2 cloves garlic, minced
2 cups ketchup
¼ cup soy sauce
¼ cup apple cider vinegar
2 tablespoons Worcestershire sauce

1 tablespoon honey
¼ cup dark brown sugar
¼ cup molasses
¼ teaspoon ground cloves
¼ teaspoon ground cinnamon
½ teaspoon fine sea salt

Heat the olive oil in a large saucepan over medium heat. Add the onion and garlic and cook for about 5 minutes, or until the onion is softened. Add the rest of the ingredients, increase the heat to medium-high, and cook, whisking frequently for 2 to 5 minutes, or until the sugar is dissolved and the sauce is smooth.

Transfer the mixture to a glass jar with a screw top, seal, and refrigerate.

Homemade Teriyaki Sauce

MAKES 1½ CUPS

2 garlic cloves, minced
2 teaspoons freshly grated
   or minced ginger
3 tablespoons mirin
1 tablespoon apple cider vinegar
6 tablespoons water

1 teaspoon sesame oil
½ cup soy sauce or tamari
3 tablespoons dark brown sugar
¼ teaspoon fine sea salt
1½ teaspoons cornstarch
1 tablespoon water or sake

Combine all the ingredients in a saucepan, except the cornstarch and water, and bring to a boil over medium-high heat. Reduce the heat to maintain a simmer and cook, stirring constantly, for 2 minutes.

In a small bowl, whisk the cornstarch and water together, and then whisk the mixture into the saucepan. Cook, whisking frequently, for 2 more minutes, or until thickened.

Transfer the mixture to a glass jar with a screw top, seal, and refrigerate.

Korean-Style Barbecue Sauce

MAKES 1 CUP

1 tablespoon neutral oil
3 large garlic cloves, finely chopped
1 (1-inch) knob fresh ginger
2 tablespoons soy sauce
¼ teaspoon fine sea salt
½ cup gochujang Korean
   red pepper paste

¼ cup dark brown sugar
1 tablespoon honey
2 tablespoons sesame oil
2 tablespoons rice vinegar
2 tablespoons sesame seeds

Heat the oil in a small saucepan over medium heat. Add the garlic, grate the ginger on a box grater right over the saucepan, and cook for 2 minutes. Add the remaining ingredients, except the sesame seeds, and cook at a low simmer, stirring frequently, for 8 minutes, or until everything is combined. Allow to cool to room temperature. Stir in the sesame seeds.

Transfer the mixture to a glass jar with a screw top, seal, and refrigerate.

Southern Mustard Barbecue Sauce

MAKES 1¾ CUPS

1 cup store-bought yellow mustard
¼ cup honey (or hot honey
   for added heat)
¼ cup dark brown sugar

¼ cup distilled white vinegar
1 tablespoon ketchup
1 teaspoon Tabasco sauce

Combine all the ingredients in a saucepan and whisk to combine. Cook over medium heat for 2 to 5 minutes, or until the ingredients are melted and combined. Taste and adjust seasonings as you wish. Allow to cool to room temperature.

Transfer the mixture to a glass jar with a screw top, seal, and refrigerate.

Japanese Barbecue Sauce (Yakiniku)

MAKES ¾ CUP

½ sweet apple, peeled, diced
2 large garlic cloves, sliced
¼ small Vidalia onion, sliced
1 tablespoon freshly grated ginger
1 tablespoon red or white miso paste
1 tablespoon honey
2 tablespoons dark brown sugar

2 teaspoons sesame oil
1 tablespoon mirin
2 tablespoons sake
2 teaspoons rice vinegar or
   apple cider vinegar
¼ cup soy sauce
½ tablespoon sesame seeds

Combine all the ingredients, except the sesame seeds, in a blender or food processor, pulse a few times, then process until smooth.

Pour into a serving bowl and garnish with sesame seeds or transfer the mixture to a glass jar with a screw top, seal, and refrigerate for up to 2 weeks.

Fresh Peach Barbecue Sauce

MAKES 2 CUPS

2 fresh peaches, peeled,
   pitted, and sliced
2 canned chipotle peppers
   in adobo sauce
¼ cup peach preserves or jam

¼ cup apple cider vinegar
1 cup store-bought ketchup
2 tablespoons dark brown sugar
1 tablespoon Dijon mustard
2 tablespoons Worcestershire sauce

Place the peaches in a food processor and process until smooth. Add the rest of the ingredients and process until smooth. If you would like the sauce thicker, cook the mixture in a saucepan over medium heat until the mixture loses some of its liquid and has thickened. Allow to cool to room temperature.

Transfer the mixture to a glass jar with a screw top, seal, and refrigerate for up to 2 weeks.

Alabama
White Barbecue Sauce

MAKES 1¼ CUPS

1 cup store-bought mayonnaise
1 tablespoon distilled white vinegar
1 teaspoon freshly ground
   black pepper
½ teaspoon fine sea salt
1 tablespoon fresh lemon juice

1 garlic clove, minced
1 teaspoon hot sauce
1 tablespoon yellow or Dijon mustard
2 teaspoons prepared horseradish
2 teaspoons Worcestershire sauce
2 teaspoons honey (optional)

Whisk together all the ingredients, including the honey, if using.

Transfer the mixture to a glass jar with a screw top, seal, and refrigerate.

Cold Dips

A DIP OR DIPPING SAUCE is a popular condiment, especially on Game Day, at the beach, or at a barbecue in the back-yard. Arrange small bowls on your condiment board in the middle of the table surrounded by bigger bowls of chips, pita triangles, tortilla chips, or veggies.

Try dipping potstickers into my addictive Kimchi-Mayonnaise Dipping Sauce (page 151) or my Vietnamese Sweet and Salty Dipping Sauce (page 158). Pile up a mountain of crispy tortilla chips next to my fresh salsas, Guacamole (page 150), and colorful Veggie Taco Layered Dip (page 156). Or swipe chunks of artisan sourdough bread through my recipe for A Cloud of Whipped Feta (page 155). All are dippable, all are delicious.

Guacamole

MAKES 2 CUPS

4 large, relatively soft avocados
1 small Vidalia onion, finely chopped
1 jalapeño pepper, seeded
   and finely chopped
1 red Fresno chile, seeded,
   finely chopped
2 medium tomatoes, finely chopped,
   reserving the seeds and juice

Juice of 1 lime
5 tablespoons fresh cilantro
   leaves, finely chopped
½ teaspoon fine sea salt
¼ teaspoon ground cumin
2 tablespoons extra-virgin olive oil

With their skin on, smash and roll the avocados on the kitchen counter so they mash up inside. You can use a rolling pin to hit them as well. Peel and scoop out the avocado into a bowl, mashing more if desired. Add all the other ingredients and mix well.

Serve or store in an airtight container in the refrigerator for up to 4 days.

Mexican-Style Black Bean Dip

MAKES 2 CUPS

1 (12-ounce) can black
   beans, drained
1 jalapeño pepper, sliced
3 large garlic cloves, sliced
¼ small red onion
Zest and juice of 1 organic lime

½ cup fresh cilantro leaves
½ teaspoon ground cumin
¼ teaspoon fine sea salt
1 teaspoon Tabasco sauce
½ cup sour cream

Combine all the ingredients in a food processor or blender and process until the consistency of a smooth dip. Adjust the seasonings to your taste.

Serve or store in an airtight container in the refrigerator for up to 1 week.

Mexican Street Corn Dip

MAKES 1½ CUPS

4 ears fresh corn on the
   cob, shucked
¼ cup mayonnaise
¼ cup sour cream
1 teaspoon granulated sugar
Zest and juice of 1 organic lime
3 garlic cloves, pressed

¼ cup cilantro leaves, minced
1 teaspoon Tabasco sauce
¼ teaspoon chili powder
   or smoked paprika
¼ teaspoon fine sea salt
½ cup crumbled queso fresco,
   feta, or goat cheese

Cook the corn on a grill for 8 to 10 minutes, or until it has grill marks. Slice the kernels off the cobs and toss them into a bowl.

In another bowl, whisk together the mayonnaise, sour cream, sugar, lime zest and juice, garlic, cilantro, Tabasco, chili powder, and salt until smooth. Add the corn kernels and crumbled cheese and gently fold them in.

Serve or store in an airtight container in the refrigerator for up to up to 4 days.

Kimchi-Mayonnaise Dipping Sauce

MAKES 1½ CUPS

1 cup mayonnaise
½ cup tightly packed store-bought red kimchi
1 tablespoon seasoned rice vinegar
   or white balsamic vinegar

Combine all the ingredients in a blender or food processor and process until smooth.

Serve or store in an airtight container in the refrigerator.

Yogurt-Cucumber Dip (Tzatziki)

MAKES 2½ CUPS

1 medium cucumber, peeled
3 large garlic cloves, peeled
    and pressed or grated
1 cup plain Greek yogurt
Juice of ½ lemon
1 teaspoon fine sea salt

½ cup sour cream
1 teaspoon hot sauce
2 tablespoons minced
    fresh mint leaves
1 tablespoon minced dill fronds

Grate the cucumber on the large holes of a box grater into a bowl. Transfer the grated cucumber to a tea towel or paper towel. Using your hands, squeeze out the liquid over the sink, and return the cucumber to the bowl. Add the garlic, yogurt, lemon juice, salt, sour cream, hot sauce, mint, and dill to the bowl and mix well to combine.

Serve or store in an airtight container in the refrigerator for up to 4 days.

Spicy Red Pepper and Feta Dip (Tirokafteri)

MAKES 1¼ CUPS

10 ounces feta, plus more as needed
2 store-bought whole roasted
    red peppers, patted dry
1 fresh red Fresno chile or jalapeño
    pepper, stemmed and sliced
1 tablespoon red wine vinegar

2 garlic cloves, sliced
2 to 3 tablespoons extra-virgin
    olive oil, plus more as needed
10 pitted kalamata olives, diced
2 tablespoons minced fresh
    Italian flat-leaf parsley leaves

Break up the feta with your hands and drop it into a food processor. Add the roasted red peppers, Fresno chile, vinegar, and garlic and process until smooth. With the machine running, drizzle in 2 tablespoons of the olive oil until the mixture is smooth and fluffy. Add the remaining 1 tablespoon if needed. Taste and adjust the seasoning.

Transfer the mixture to a serving bowl, drizzle with olive oil in a circle around the perimeter and scatter with kalamata olives and parsley.

The dip can be stored in an airtight container in the refrigerator for up to 4 days.

Greek Whipped Potato and Garlic Dip (Skordalia)

MAKES 2 TO 3 CUPS

1 pound russet or gold potatoes, peeled and cubed
1 teaspoon fine sea salt
5 large garlic cloves, sliced
3 ounces walnuts
¼ cup freshly squeezed lemon juice

¾ to 1 cup extra-virgin olive oil, plus more if needed
Zest of ½ lemon
2 tablespoons minced fresh Italian flat-leaf parsley leaves
1 tablespoon coarse sea salt flakes

Combine the potatoes with enough water to cover in a large pot and bring to a boil over medium-high heat. Reduce the heat to maintain a rapid simmer and cook for 10 to 15 minutes, or until the potatoes are very soft. Reserve ½ cup of the cooking water. Drain the potatoes in a colander over the sink and let sit for 5 minutes to allow the moisture to evaporate before tossing them into a food processor.

Add the salt, garlic, walnuts, and lemon juice and process until well combined. With the machine running, add ¾ cup of oil in a thin stream. Add the remaining ¼ cup oil, if needed, until you reach the consistency you desire. If you would like a thinner dip, add the reserved cooking water, more lemon juice, or more oil, 1 tablespoon at a time. You are looking for a fluffy smooth dip. Taste and adjust seasoning.

Transfer the mixture to a serving bowl. Garnish with a drizzle of olive oil, the lemon zest, minced parsley, and a scattering of coarse sea salt flakes

The dip can be stored in an airtight container in the refrigerator for up to 1 week.

South of France Rouille Dip

MAKES ¾ CUP

5 large garlic cloves, peeled
1 store-bought roasted red
   pepper from a jar
1 small fresh red Fresno chile,
   seeded and sliced
1 large egg yolk, room temperature

1 teaspoon fine sea salt
1 slice white bread, crusts
   removed, torn into pieces
1 ½ tablespoons freshly
   squeezed lemon juice
½ cup extra-virgin olive oil

With the food processor running, drop in the garlic to mince. Turn off the food processor, add the roasted red pepper, Fresno chile, egg yolk, salt, bread, and lemon juice, and process for 60 seconds.

With the machine running, add the olive oil very slowly, until it reaches a mayonnaise consistency. Transfer to a serving bowl.

The dip can be stored in an airtight container in the refrigerator for up to 1 week.

Provençal Red Pepper Dip (Poivronade)

MAKES 2 CUPS

2 large red bell peppers
2 large garlic cloves
3 tablespoons slivered almonds
1 cup grated Parmesan cheese
¼ teaspoon smoked paprika
   or piment d'Espelette,
   plus more if needed

10 fresh basil leaves
2 tablespoons extra-virgin olive
   oil, plus more as needed
2 tablespoons freshly
   squeezed lemon juice
Fine sea salt, if desired

Preheat the oven to 350 degrees F. Line a baking sheet with parchment paper or aluminum foil.

Put the bell peppers on the baking sheet and bake for 25 minutes. Flip the peppers over and bake for another 15 to 20 minutes, until they are very soft. Allow the peppers to cool to room temperature.

Peel the peppers. Discard the stem and seeds or keep them. Cut the peppers into big chunks.

With the food processor running, drop the garlic and almonds through the tube and process until finely ground. Add the cheese, paprika, basil, olive oil and lemon juice and pulse until smooth. Add the roasted red peppers and process until very smooth. Add a drizzle of olive oil, if needed, and process again until the mixture is smooth and spreadable. Taste and add salt if desired.

Transfer the mixture to a serving bowl and garnish with a dash of smoked paprika and a drizzle of olive oil.

The dip can be stored in an airtight container in the refrigerator.

A Cloud of Whipped Feta

MAKES 2 CUPS

1 (8-ounce) block feta
½ cup mayonnaise
½ cup sour cream or
   plain Greek yogurt
1 large garlic clove, sliced
Zest and juice of ½ organic lemon

¼ teaspoon fine sea salt
1 teaspoon dried basil
2 tablespoons extra-virgin olive oil
¼ cup honey
1 tablespoon minced walnuts

Break the feta into a food processor and pulse until crumbled. Add the mayonnaise, sour cream, garlic, lemon zest and juice, salt, basil, and oil and process until very smooth. Transfer to a serving bowl.

In a small bowl, mix the honey and walnuts together. Make a well in the center of the feta dip and spoon the honey and walnut mixture into it.

The dip can be stored in an airtight container in the refrigerator for up to 1 week.

Whipped Pistachio and Feta Dip

MAKES 2 CUPS

1 cup pistachios, divided
¾ cup crumbled feta
3 tablespoons extra-virgin olive
    oil, plus more as needed

½ cup plain Greek yogurt
Zest of ½ organic lemon
¼ teaspoon coarse sea salt flakes

Combine ¾ cup of the pistachios in a food processor and process until finely ground. Add the feta, oil, yogurt, and lemon zest and process until very smooth.

Transfer the mixture to a serving bowl. Scatter the remaining ¼ cup pistachios around the edges and drizzle some olive oil on top of the pistachios. Scatter the sea salt flakes over the top.

The dip can be stored in an airtight container in the refrigerator for up to 1 week.

Veggie Taco Layered Dip

MAKES ABOUT 4 CUPS

2 (8-ounce) packages cream cheese,
    softened and cut into pieces
16 ounces sour cream
1 ½ (1-ounce) packets
    taco seasoning
1 teaspoon ground cumin
Juice of 1 lime
Fine sea salt, as needed
½ small red onion, finely diced

1 small green bell pepper,
    seeded and finely diced
2 medium tomatoes, diced
1 avocado, pitted, peeled, and diced
1 (2 ¼-ounce) can sliced black olives
1 (4-ounce) can diced
    jalapeño peppers
Hot sauce, of choice
1 cup grated cheddar cheese

Combine the cream cheese, sour cream, taco seasoning, cumin, and lime juice in a blender and process until very smooth. Taste and add salt at this point, if needed. Spread out the mixture on a serving dish or platter.

Scatter the red onion over the top. Then scatter the bell pepper in a layer, and then the tomato in a layer. Scatter the avocado over the tomato layer. Then scatter the olives in a layer. Then scatter the jalapeños over the olives. Sprinkle some hot sauce over the top and finally, sprinkle the grated cheese all over the top.

The dip can be stored in an airtight container in the refrigerator for up to 3 days.

Cilantro and Mango Salsa

MAKES 3 CUPS

2 ripe tomatoes
2 ripe mangoes, peeled
Zest and juice of 1 organic lime
¼ teaspoon ground cumin
1 teaspoon granulated sugar

½ teaspoon fine sea salt, plus more as needed
¼ teaspoon hot sauce, plus more as needed
½ cup chopped fresh cilantro leaves

Cut the tomatoes in half, seed them, squeeze out any juice, then finely chop. Transfer to a bowl.

Cut the flesh off the mangoes, finely chop, and transfer to the bowl of tomatoes.

Add 1 tablespoon lime zest, the lime juice, cumin, sugar, salt, and hot sauce and stir well to coat. Taste and add more salt or hot sauce if desired. Stir in the cilantro leaves.

Serve or store in an airtight container in the refrigerator for up to 3 days.

Fresh Peach Salsa

MAKES 2 CUPS

2 firm peaches, peeled and
cut into ¼-inch dice
2 ripe peaches, peeled and
cut into ¼-inch dice
2 tablespoons freshly
squeezed lemon juice
1 large tomato, peeled and
cut into ¼-in dice
½ small red onion, cut
into ¼-inch dice

½ fresh jalapeño pepper,
finely chopped
3 tablespoons fresh cilantro
leaves, finely chopped
½ cup olive oil
2 tablespoons honey
5 tablespoons white balsamic
vinegar (or rice vinegar)
¼ teaspoon fine sea salt

Combine the peaches and lemon juice in a bowl
and toss to thoroughly coat. Add the tomato,
onion, jalapeño, and cilantro and stir to
combine.

In a small bowl, combine the olive oil,
honey, vinegar, and salt and whisk well.
Pour the mixture over the peach mixture
and stir well to coat.

Serve or store in an airtight container in the
refrigerator for up to 3 days.

Vietnamese Sweet and Salty Dipping Sauce

MAKES 1½ CUPS

2 organic limes, ½ lime zested
first, then all juiced
1 cup water

1 tablespoon Asian fish sauce,
plus more as needed
2 teaspoons rice wine vinegar

4 tablespoons white sugar,
 plus more as needed
2 large garlic cloves, pressed

1 small jalapeño pepper or red
 Fresno chile, seeded and minced
½ small carrot, grated
 on a box grater

Whisk together all the ingredients, except the carrots, in a saucepan over medium heat and cook, whisking constantly, for about 5 minutes, or until the sugar is dissolved and the flavors meld together. Check for seasoning and add more of any ingredient to your taste. Take the pan off the heat and stir in the carrot.

The dipping sauce can be stored in an airtight container in the refrigerator for up to 1 week.

Rémoulade Dipping Sauce

MAKES 1¼ CUPS

2 egg yolks, room temperature
2 teaspoons Dijon mustard
¼ teaspoon fine sea salt,
 plus more as needed
½ teaspoon granulated sugar
½ cup vegetable oil
½ cup extra-virgin olive oil

1 tablespoon distilled white
 vinegar or tarragon vinegar
2 tablespoons capers,
 finely chopped
4 cornichons or tiny dill
 pickles, finely chopped
2 sprigs fresh tarragon, leaves
 only, finely chopped

Combine the egg yolks, mustard, salt, and sugar in the bowl of a stand mixer and beat for about 1 minute, or until pale yellow and thick. With the mixer running, drip in the oils, drop by drop, for about 40 seconds. Then drizzle the oil in a very thin stream until you achieve the consistency of mayonnaise. Beat in the vinegar until well mixed. Stir in the capers, cornichons, and tarragon. Taste and add more salt, if desired.

The dipping sauce can be stored in an airtight container in the refrigerator for up to 3 days.

Hot Dips

YOU CAN PRESENT one big hot dip in a standard size fondue pot on a condiment board for people to gather around, or present three or four dips in smaller bowls or sitting over individual butter warmers.

From a vintage dip like Baked Artichoke, Crab, and Spinach Dip (page 162) to an anchovy-forward Bagna Càuda (page 164) served with a gorgeous display of crisp vegetables, these cozy dips are to be shared.

Baked Artichoke, Crab, and Spinach Dip

MAKES 4 CUPS

2 tablespoons unsalted butter, plus more as needed
10 ounces fresh spinach
4 garlic cloves finely chopped
1 ½ cups coarsely chopped canned or jarred artichoke hearts
⅔ cup heavy cream
4 ounces cream cheese

½ teaspoon fine sea salt
¼ teaspoon cayenne pepper
8 ounces lump crabmeat or chopped shrimp, drained and squeezed dry
8 ounces mozzarella cheese
⅔ cup freshly grated Parmesan cheese

Preheat the oven to 375 degrees F. Generously butter a 1 ½-quart baking dish.

Melt the butter in a skillet over medium heat. Add all of the spinach at once and cook until wilted down. Add the garlic and artichokes and cook, stirring, for 4 minutes.

Reduce the heat to low, add the cream, cream cheese, salt, and cayenne pepper, and cook, stirring, until the cream cheese is melted and everything is combined. Stir in the crabmeat.

Grate the mozzarella on the large holes of a box grater right over the crabmeat in the skillet. Increase the heat to medium and cook, stirring, until the mozzarella melts into the mixture.

Transfer the mixture to the baking dish, sprinkle the Parmesan cheese over the top, and bake for 20 to 25 minutes, or until golden brown and bubbly.

The dip can be stored in an airtight container in the refrigerator for up to 4 days.

Roasted Garlic, Bacon, and Gruyère Fondue

MAKES 2 CUPS

1 whole garlic bulb
Olive oil, for drizzling
6 slices bacon
1 cup dry white wine
1 tablespoon brandy

¼ teaspoon ground nutmeg
⅓ pound Gruyère cheese
⅓ pound fontina cheese
⅓ pound Emmental cheese
2 tablespoons cornstarch

Preheat the oven to 400 degrees F.

Cut the garlic in half horizontally. Place the garlic on a piece of aluminum foil, drizzle with oil, and close the foil into a packet. Place the packet in the oven and bake for 25 minutes. Allow to cool to room temperature.

While the garlic is baking, fry the bacon until crispy, drain on paper towels, then crumble and set aside.

Combine the wine, brandy, and nutmeg in a large saucepan, fondue pot, or cast-iron skillet and bring to a simmer over medium-high heat. Squeeze the garlic out of its skin right into the pan.

Grate the cheeses on a box grater into a bowl. Sprinkle the cheese with the cornstarch and toss it with your hands to coat. Add the cheese mixture to the saucepan and cook, stirring constantly, until the cheese is melted and very smooth.

To serve, sprinkle the top with the crumbled bacon.

The dip can be stored in an airtight container in the refrigerator for up to 4 days.

Spreads

WHAT IS THE DIFFERENCE between a dip and a spread? For me, a spread is swiped onto food with a knife, while dips have food dipped into them. Yet, I have included several hummus recipes here because I personally spread it on little pitas or sandwiches, while others may dip their pita into it.

I serve a few spreads on a condiment board and offer it to guests before they sit down to dinner or include them on an appetizer buffet.

Traditional Hummus

MAKES 2 CUPS

2 large garlic cloves
⅔ cup tahini
½ cup freshly squeezed lemon juice
½ teaspoon fine sea salt

2 teaspoons ground cumin
1 (15-ounce) can chickpeas, drained
Extra-virgin olive oil

Combine the garlic, tahini, lemon juice, salt, cumin, and chickpeas in a food processor or blender and process until smooth. Add a bit of water if the hummus is too thick and process again. Taste for seasoning. Transfer to a serving bowl, drizzle olive oil around the perimeter, and serve.

The hummus can be stored in an airtight container in the refrigerator for up to 1 week.

Holiday Pumpkin Hummus

MAKES 3 CUPS

1 (15-ounce) can chickpeas
   or white beans, drained
1 cup canned pumpkin purée
1 tablespoon freshly
   squeezed lemon juice
2 tablespoons extra-virgin olive oil

2 tablespoons tahini
1 tablespoon honey
1 teaspoon fine sea salt
1 teaspoon pumpkin pie spice
2 tablespoons pumpkin seeds

Combine all the ingredients, except the pumpkin seeds, in a food processor and process until very smooth. If the mixture is too thick, add cold water or oil, 1 tablespoon at a time, and process until it reaches the desired consistency. Transfer to a serving bowl, sprinkle the pumpkin seeds around the perimeter, and serve.

The hummus can be stored in an airtight container in the refrigerator for up to 1 week.

Zucchini and Pistachio Hummus

MAKES 1½ CUPS

5 tablespoons extra-virgin olive oil, plus
    more as needed, divided
2 medium zucchini, cut into thin slices
    then coarsely chopped
1 garlic clove, minced
1⅓ cups canned chickpeas, drained
⅓ cup plus ¼ cup shelled salted pistachios
½ teaspoon fine sea salt

Heat 2 tablespoons of the oil in a large skillet over medium heat. Add the zucchini and garlic and cook for 5 to 7 minutes, or until the zucchini is just tender. Transfer the mixture into a food processor or blender.

Add the remaining 3 tablespoons of oil, chickpeas, ⅓ cup of pistachios, and salt and process until very smooth. Transfer the mixture to a serving bowl and drizzle with olive oil. Coarsely chop the remaining ¼ cup of pistachios and sprinkle them over the top.

The hummus can be stored in an airtight container in the refrigerator for up to 3 days.

Black and Green Tapenade

MAKES 1 CUP

½ cup kalamata olives, pitted
½ cup green olives with pimientos
7 anchovy fillets, plus 3
    teaspoons of the oil
1 tablespoon capers, drained
½ teaspoon herbes de Provence
2 tablespoons extra-virgin olive oil

Combine all the ingredients in a food processor and process until it is a smooth paste. Transfer to a ramekin or small bowl to serve.

The spread can be stored in an airtight container in the refrigerator.

Onion Confit Spread

MAKES 1½ CUPS

3 tablespoons extra-virgin olive oil
2 medium white onions,
   finely minced

2 teaspoons minced fresh rosemary
1 teaspoon fine sea salt

Heat the olive oil in a skillet over medium heat. Add the onions and rosemary and cook, stirring frequently for 20 to 30 minutes, or until the onions are lightly colored and soft. Stir in the salt. Taste and adjust seasoning. Spoon the mixture into a serving bowl.

The spread can be stored in an airtight container in the refrigerator for up to 4 days.

Fresh Basil Hummus with Tahini Sauce

MAKES ALMOST 2 CUPS

FOR THE HUMMUS
1 (15-ounce) can chickpeas, reserve
   the liquid and 4 chickpeas
2 tablespoons extra-virgin olive
   oil, plus more as needed
½ tablespoon freshly
   squeezed lemon juice
½ teaspoon balsamic vinegar
1 cup tightly packed fresh basil
   leaves, plus 2 tablespoons minced
2 tablespoons chopped
   walnuts or pine nuts
3 garlic cloves, sliced
¼ teaspoon fine sea salt
¼ cup water

FOR THE TAHINI SAUCE
½ cup pourable tahini
¼ cup freshly squeezed lemon juice
1 tablespoon extra-virgin olive oil
½ teaspoon fine sea salt
⅛ teaspoon ground cumin
2 large garlic cloves,
   minced or grated

To make the hummus, heat the oil in a saucepan over medium heat. Add the chickpeas and the liquid from the can and cook about 1 minute, or until hot. Drain and transfer to a food processor. Add oil, lemon juice, vinegar, 1 cup basil, walnuts, garlic, and salt and process until smooth. If needed, add the water, 1 tablespoon at a time, to thin out the hummus or make it smoother. Transfer to a serving bowl.

To make the tahini sauce, whisk together all the ingredients in a bowl.

To finish the hummus, spoon the tahini sauce around the top of the hummus. Drizzle with olive oil, top with the 4 reserved chickpeas, and scatter the minced basil leaves and serve.

The hummus and sauce can be stored in an airtight container in the refrigerator for up to 3 days.

Baba Ghanouj

MAKES 3 CUPS

2 medium globe eggplants
4 large garlic cloves
¼ cup freshly squeezed lemon juice
½ cup tahini
½ teaspoon fine sea salt

¼ teaspoon ground cumin
1 teaspoon smoked paprika
3 tablespoons mayonnaise
1 tablespoon extra-virgin olive oil

Preheat the oven to 375 degrees F.

Pierce the eggplants all over and put them on a baking sheet. Bake for 20 minutes. Turn the eggplants over and bake for 25 to 30 minutes more, or until they are very soft. Allow to cool to room temperature.

Cut the eggplants in half, scoop out the flesh, and transfer it to a food processor. Add the garlic, lemon juice, tahini, salt, cumin, paprika, mayonnaise, and olive oil and process until smooth. Taste and adjust seasoning.

The spread can be stored in an airtight container in the refrigerator for up to 4 days.

Whipped Camembert

MAKES 1 CUP

1 (8-ounce) wheel Camembert, room
  temperature, cut into small dice
2 tablespoons heavy cream
1 tablespoon honey

¼ teaspoon fine sea salt
2 tablespoons fresh thyme leaves
1 tablespoon minced dried
  apricots (optional)

In a bowl with a handheld electric mixer or in a stand mixer, whip the
diced Camembert until it has broken down and is creamy. Add the cream,
honey, and salt, and whip again until light and fluffy. Taste and adjust the
seasonings, as desired. Transfer the mixture to a serving bowl.

Garnish with thyme leaves and minced apricots, if using.

The spread can be stored in an airtight container in the refrigerator for up
to 2 weeks.

Homemade Red Caviar Spread (Taramosalata)

MAKES 2 CUPS

4 slices sourdough bread,
  crusts removed
Whole milk, room temperature
1 garlic clove
1 tablespoon freshly
  squeezed lemon juice
¼ teaspoon sweet paprika
½ cup red fish roe or red
  salmon caviar
1 cup extra-virgin olive oil
Fine sea salt
2 tablespoons seltzer
  water (optional)

2 tablespoons minced red onion
½ cup minced smoked
  salmon (optional)

Place the bread slices in a shallow bowl and add enough milk to cover. Let soak for 60 seconds. With your hands, squeeze the liquid out of the bread and transfer the bread to a food processor.

Add the garlic, lemon juice, paprika, and fish roe and process until very smooth. With the machine running, pour the oil, drop by drop, into the mixture for about 30 seconds. Then pour the rest of the oil in a very thin stream until the mixture is thick and spreadable. Taste and add some salt or other seasonings to your taste and pulse to blend again. Add the seltzer, if using, and blend again. The seltzer will make the mixture lighter. Fold in the minced onion and minced salmon, if using, and blend well. Transfer to a small bowl and serve. The spread can be stored in an airtight container in the refrigerator for up to 4 days.

Bavarian Cheese Spread

MAKES 2 CUPS

9 ounces Camembert cheese, room temperature, cubed
6 ounces cream cheese or Laughing Cow cheese, room temperature, cubed
5 tablespoons unsalted butter, softened
1 teaspoon yellow or Dijon mustard
3 teaspoons sweet paprika
½ teaspoon ground caraway seeds
3 tablespoons dark beer, plus more as needed
Fine sea salt, as needed
Freshly ground black pepper, as needed
½ small red onion, finely chopped
1 tablespoon minced chives
Whole milk, as needed

Combine the Camembert, cream cheese, butter, mustard, paprika, caraway, and beer into a food processor and pulse until blended but still a bit chunky. Taste for seasoning, add salt or pepper, and adjust as desired. Fold in the onion and chives. Transfer to an airtight container and refrigerate for at least 5 hours or overnight before serving. If you would like it to be more like a dip, stir in a bit more beer or some milk.

The spread can be refrigerated for up to 1 month.

Pink Beet and Feta Spread

MAKES 1¼ CUPS

⅓ cup cooked vacuum-packed
   beets or canned beets, chopped
2 large garlic cloves, sliced
½ teaspoon fine sea salt
1 teaspoon Dijon mustard

¼ teaspoon ground nutmeg
8 ounces crumbled feta,
   room temperature
1 tablespoon extra-virgin olive oil

Combine all the ingredients into a food processor or blender and process for about 4 minutes, until light and fluffy.

The spread can be stored in an airtight container in the refrigerator for up to 1 week.

Roquefort and Cream Cheese Spread

MAKES 1 CUP

1 (4-ounce) package cream
   cheese, softened
4 ounces Roquefort or blue cheese
½ small onion

1 tablespoon Worcestershire sauce
1 tablespoon minced fresh chives
Freshly ground black pepper
Fine sea salt, as needed

Combine the cream cheese and Roquefort in a food processor and pulse until blended.

On the large holes of a box grater, grate the onion directly onto the cheese. Add the Worcestershire sauce, chives, and black pepper and pulse until smooth. Taste and add salt if desired. Transfer to a serving bowl.

The spread can be stored in an airtight container in the refrigerator for up to 1 month.

Avocado and Feta Dip

MAKES 1½ CUPS

8 ounces crumbled feta,
   room temperature
1 ripe avocado, pitted, peeled,
   and coarsely chopped
¼ teaspoon fine sea salt

2 tablespoons extra-virgin olive
   oil, plus more as needed
1 sprig fresh oregano,
   leaves only (optional)

Pulse the feta in a food processor 6 times. Add the avocado chunks and process for about 4 minutes, or until very creamy. Add the salt and olive oil and process again until well combined and fluffy. Transfer to a serving bowl and swirl the top with a drizzle of olive oil and oregano if using.

The spread can be stored in an airtight container in the refrigerator for up to 3 days.

Spreadable
Cherry Tomato Confit

MAKES ABOUT 2 CUPS

2 pints cherry tomatoes, stemmed
6 large garlic cloves, thickly sliced
1 cup extra-virgin olive oil
2 teaspoons granulated sugar

½ teaspoon fine sea salt
2 sprigs fresh rosemary, leaves
   only, coarsely chopped

Combine all the ingredients in a saucepan over low heat and simmer, stirring frequently, for 35 to 45 minutes, or until the tomatoes are wrinkled. Allow to cool.

Transfer to clean glass jars with screw tops and seal. Use immediately or store in the refrigerator for up to 4 days. The oil will thicken from the cold, so bring to room temperature before using.

Spreadable Garlic Confit

MAKES 2 CUPS

6 whole garlic heads
2 cups extra-virgin olive oil
1 teaspoon coarsely chopped
   fresh rosemary

½ teaspoon fine sea salt
1 to 2 fresh rosemary sprigs

Peel all the cloves of garlic and place them in a saucepan over low heat. Add the oil, chopped rosemary, and salt and cook for about 35 minutes, or until the garlic cloves are very soft. Allow to cool in the saucepan to room temperature.

Transfer the garlic and oil to clean glass jars with screw tops. Tuck 1 rosemary sprig into each jar and seal.

Use immediately or store in the refrigerator for up to 1 week. The oil will thicken from the cold, so bring to room temperature before using.

Just-Like-Pizza Spread

MAKES 1¼ CUPS

¼ cup plus 1 tablespoon sun-
   dried tomatoes in oil, drained
   and minced, divided
4 thin slices pepperoni, minced
1 (8-ounce) package cream
   cheese, softened
1 teaspoon dried oregano
¼ teaspoon garlic powder
¼ teaspoon onion powder

⅛ teaspoon crushed red
   pepper flakes
¼ teaspoon fine sea salt
⅛ teaspoon coarse sea salt flakes

Combine the ¼ cup sun-dried tomatoes, pepperoni, cream cheese, oregano, garlic powder, onion powder, red pepper flakes, and salt in a bowl and beat with a handheld mixer until well combined and fluffy. Chill for 2 hours, until the flavors meld.

Scatter the remaining 1 tablespoon minced sun-dried tomatoes over the top, sprinkle with the coarse sea salt flakes, and serve.

The spread can be stored in an airtight container in the refrigerator.

Warm Salmon, Wine, and Shallots Spread

MAKES 2 TO 3 CUPS

1 pound fresh salmon
8 tablespoons unsalted butter,
    plus more as needed,
    room temperature
½ teaspoon fine sea salt,
    plus more as needed
Freshly ground black pepper
4 tablespoons plus ½ teaspoon
    white wine vinegar, divided

3 large shallots, finely chopped
½ cup Muscadet wine or
    dry white wine
2 teaspoons freshly
    squeezed lemon juice
1 ½ tablespoons finely chopped
    fresh tarragon leaves

Preheat the broiler. Dot the salmon with a little butter, salt, and pepper, place on a baking sheet, and broil for about 5 minutes, until just cooked. Transfer to the bowl of a stand mixer and flake the salmon with a fork.

Heat 4 tablespoons of vinegar in a saucepan over medium heat. Add the shallots, ½ teaspoon salt, and wine and cook until there is very little liquid left. Reduce the heat to low, stir in the 8 tablespoons of butter, a little at a time, and cook until melted. Sprinkle in the remaining ½ teaspoon of vinegar, lemon juice, and tarragon and stir again. Season with salt and pepper. Add the mixture to the salmon and beat for 30 seconds, or until it's combined and becomes spreadable. Transfer to a serving bowl or ramekin.

The spread can be stored in an airtight container in the refrigerator for up to 4 days.

Ginger and Apricot Cream Cheese Spread

MAKES 1 CUP

1 (8-ounce) package cream cheese, softened
2 tablespoons ginger jam or ginger preserves

¼ cup finely chopped dried apricots
1 tablespoon honey
¼ teaspoon fine sea salt

Combine all the ingredients in a food processor and process until smooth. Taste and add more of any of the ingredients to taste. Transfer the mixture to a small bowl to serve.

The spread can be stored in an airtight container in the refrigerator.

Cashew or Peanut Butter

MAKES 2 CUPS

2 cups unsalted cashews or peanuts
2 tablespoons neutral oil

Fine sea salt

Heat the oven to 300 degrees F.

Spread out the cashews on a baking sheet. Bake for about 6 minutes. Allow to cool to room temperature.

Transfer the cashews to a food processor and process for 4 minutes. With the machine running, slowly stream in the oil until you reach the consistency you want. Add salt, to taste, and pulse 4 times to blend.

The spread can be stored in an airtight container in the refrigerator for up to 1 month.

Before serving, bring to room temperature and stir the cashew butter as the oil might separate from the solids.

Chocolate-Hazelnut Spread

MAKES 2 CUPS

2 cups raw hazelnuts or unsalted roasted hazelnuts

2 tablespoons brown sugar

2 tablespoons confectioners' sugar, plus more if needed

1 tablespoon unsweetened dark cocoa powder

1 teaspoon vanilla extract

2 tablespoons vegetable oil, coconut oil, or hazelnut oil

¼ teaspoon fine sea salt

1 teaspoon ground cinnamon (optional)

6 ounces dark chocolate, chopped, melted

6 ounces milk chocolate, chopped, melted

If the hazelnuts have skins on them, spread them out on a baking sheet and bake them in a 375-degree F oven for 15 minutes to bring out their oils. Rub the hazelnuts in a kitchen towel to remove the skins. You won't remove all the skins but you'll remove most of them.

If you are using unsalted roasted hazelnuts, skip this step.

Process the hazelnuts into a food processor until the mixture has the consistency of peanut butter. This could take up to 10 minutes and you may have to stop and scrape down the sides a couple of times.

Add the brown sugar, confectioners' sugar, cocoa powder, vanilla, oil, salt, and cinnamon, if using, and process until smooth.

Add the dark and milk chocolate to the food processor and process until well blended and smooth. Taste and add more sugar if needed. Transfer to an airtight container. It can be stored at room temperature for at least 1 week or in the refrigerator for up to 3 weeks.

Cold Sauces

Absolutely! I swirl them in the center of soups or layer them with a dollop on top of another sauce to add flavor. Sometimes I spoon pesto sauce over pasta dressed with tomato sauce. I drape sauces over a pork chop or slices of steak. If condiments adorn and embellish, sauces certainly do!

Shrimp Cocktail Sauce

MAKES 1¼ CUPS

1 cup ketchup
¼ cup prepared horseradish
1 tablespoon freshly
   squeezed lemon juice

1 tablespoon freshly
   squeezed lime juice
½ teaspoon hot sauce
¼ teaspoon fine sea salt
1 teaspoon Worcestershire sauce

Combine all the ingredients in a bowl and whisk to combine. Cover and refrigerate until cold.

The sauce can be stored in the refrigerator.

Homemade Worcestershire Sauce

MAKES 1 CUP

1 cup distilled white vinegar
2 tablespoons dark brown sugar
2 tablespoons tamarind paste
3 tablespoons tamari or soy sauce
½ teaspoon ground dry mustard
1 teaspoon finely ground black pepper
¼ cup molasses

½ teaspoon ground cloves
½ teaspoon onion powder
1 teaspoon ground ginger
½ teaspoon ground allspice
2 cloves garlic, pressed
2 oil-packed anchovy fillets, minced
¼ teaspoon ground cinnamon

Combine all the ingredients in a saucepan and bring to a boil over medium-high heat. Reduce the heat to maintain a simmer and cook, whisking frequently, for 15 minutes. Taste and adjust seasoning to your desired level.

Allow to cool to room temperature. If you like, you can strain this through cheesecloth or a fine-mesh strainer into jars, but it is not necessary.

Transfer to an airtight container and refrigerate for up to 2 months.

Bang Bang Sauce

MAKES 1 CUP

⅓ cup Thai sweet chili sauce
½ cup mayonnaise
2 teaspoons sriracha
½ teaspoon garlic powder
3 teaspoons honey

1 teaspoon rice wine vinegar
¼ teaspoon fine sea salt

Whisk together all the ingredients
in a bowl. Transfer to a serving
bowl and serve. Store to an airtight
container and refrigerate.

Korean Spicy Sauce (Ssamjang)

MAKES ½ CUP

1 jalapeño pepper, stemmed
  and sliced
2 garlic cloves
¼ cup chopped red onion
2 tablespoons honey
2 tablespoons sesame oil
2 tablespoons Gochujang paste
  (Korean chili paste)

1 tablespoon white miso paste
1 (¼-inch) knob fresh ginger,
  peeled and sliced
Water, as needed
1 scallion, minced, plus
  more as needed
1 tablespoon plus 1 teaspoon
  sesame seeds, divided

Combine the jalapeño, garlic, onion, honey, sesame oil, Gochujang, miso,
and ginger in a food processor or blender and process until smooth. Add a
bit of water to thin it out, if needed. Stir in the scallion and 1 tablespoon of
sesame seeds.

Transfer to a serving bowl and garnish with minced scallions and the
remaining 1 teaspoon of sesame seeds.

Transfer to an airtight container and refrigerate.

Crème Fraîche Tartare Sauce

MAKES 1¼ CUPS

½ cup mayonnaise
½ cup crème fraîche
2 tablespoons minced rinsed capers
2 tablespoons minced cornichons
1 garlic clove, minced
1 teaspoon Dijon mustard

⅛ teaspoon fine sea salt
2 teaspoons freshly
    squeezed lemon juice
½ teaspoon Tabasco sauce
2 teaspoons minced fresh
    tarragon leaves

Combine all the ingredients in a bowl and mix well. Taste for seasoning. Cover and refrigerate for 3 hours before using. Transfer to an airtight container and refrigerate for up to 4 days.

Sauce Vierge

MAKES 1½ CUPS

½ cup extra-virgin olive oil,
    plus more as needed
1 teaspoon Dijon mustard
3 medium tomatoes, finely chopped,
    reserving the juice and seeds
Zest and juice of 1 organic lemon
2 garlic cloves, minced
1 tablespoon drained
    capers, chopped

1 small shallot, minced
2 tablespoons minced
    fresh basil leaves
1 tablespoon minced fresh Italian
    flat-leaf parsley leaves
½ teaspoon fine sea salt
16 large pitted green olives,
    coarsely chopped
8 cherry tomatoes, quartered

Combine the olive oil and mustard and whisk until cloudy. Add the chopped tomatoes, 2 tablespoons of lemon juice, lemon zest, garlic, capers, shallot, basil, parsley, and salt and stir to combine. Add the olives and cherry tomatoes and stir to combine. Stir in more olive oil if you would like it thinner, and serve.

Transfer to an airtight container and refrigerate for up to 4 days.

Classic Mignonette Sauce

MAKES ⅔ CUP

1 medium shallot, finely minced
⅓ cup red wine vinegar

¼ teaspoon fine sea salt

Combine all the ingredients in a bowl and mix well.

Transfer to a clean glass jar with a screw top, seal, and refrigerate for at least 1 hour before serving and up to 2 weeks.

Fresh Mint Sauce

MAKES 1 CUP

¼ cup water
1 cup minced fresh mint leaves
1 ½ tablespoons
    confectioners' sugar

⅛ teaspoon fine sea salt
2 tablespoons apple cider vinegar

Bring the water to a boil in a small saucepan over medium-high heat.

Place the mint leaves in a bowl, pour in the boiling water, and muddle or press the mint with the back of a spoon. Add the sugar, salt, and vinegar and whisk to combine. Add more water, if needed, to thin out. Let sit at room temperature for 2 hours before serving.

Transfer to an airtight container and refrigerate for up to 2 days.

Famous Burger or Fish Sandwich Sauce

MAKES 1¾ CUPS

1 cup mayonnaise
6 tablespoons ketchup
¼ teaspoon Tabasco
   sauce or hot sauce
½ teaspoon fine sea salt

2 ½ teaspoons yellow mustard
1 teaspoon apple cider vinegar
1 teaspoon distilled white vinegar
5 tablespoons sweet relish

Whisk together all the ingredients in a bowl. Transfer to an airtight container and refrigerate.

Canary Islands Mojo Red Pepper Sauce

MAKES 1½ CUPS

2 large red bell peppers,
   seeded, coarsely diced
3 large garlic cloves, sliced
1 small green jalapeño pepper, cut
   into coarse dice including seeds
2 tablespoons red wine vinegar,
   plus more as needed

1 tablespoon ground cumin
1 teaspoon sweet paprika
½ teaspoon fine sea salt
4 tablespoons extra-virgin olive
   oil, plus more as needed
1 slice white bread, crusts
   removed, coarsely chopped

Combine the bell peppers, garlic, jalapeño, vinegar, cumin, and salt in a blender or food processor and process until smooth but not too liquid. Add the olive oil and bread pieces and process until smooth. Add a bit more olive oil or vinegar if desired.

Transfer to an airtight container and refrigerate for up to 4 days.

Chimichurri

MAKES 1½ CUPS

1 cup tightly packed fresh parsley
½ cup tightly packed fresh
   cilantro leaves
1 teaspoon dried oregano
1 small shallot, peeled
3 large garlic cloves
2 tablespoons red wine vinegar

1 fresh red Fresno chile,
   seeded and minced
½ teaspoon fine sea salt
¼ teaspoon freshly ground
   black pepper
½ cup extra-virgin olive oil

Combine the parsley, cilantro, oregano, shallot, and garlic in a food processor and process for about 15 seconds, or until well chopped. Transfer to a bowl. Add all the other ingredients, stir well, and serve.

Transfer to an airtight container and refrigerate for up to 1 week.

Anchovy Pesto Sauce

MAKES 2 CUPS

3 large garlic cloves
¼ cup fresh parsley leaves
¼ cup fresh basil leaves
3 (2-ounce) cans anchovies,
   with their oil

2 tablespoons distilled white vinegar
2 tablespoons freshly
   squeezed lemon juice
1 cup fresh white breadcrumbs
¾ cup extra-virgin olive oil

With the food processor running, drop the garlic through the tube and process until minced. Add the parsley, basil, anchovies and their oil, vinegar, lemon juice, and breadcrumbs and process until smooth.

With the machine running, drizzle in a thin stream of the oil until the pesto is creamy and thick. If it is too thick, add a bit of water and pulse. Taste for seasoning and adjust.

Transfer to an airtight container and refrigerate for up to 4 days.

Lemon Pesto Sauce

MAKES ¾ CUP

Juice of 2 large organic lemons,
   plus the zest of ½ lemon
½ cup extra-virgin olive oil
4 ounces Parmesan or
   Pecorino Romano cheese,
   cut into small chunks

4 ounces pine nuts,
   walnuts, or almonds
4 sprigs fresh basil, leaves only
2 garlic cloves
1 teaspoon fine sea salt

Combine all the ingredients in a food processor or blender and process until smooth. Taste and adjust seasonings.

Transfer to an airtight container and refrigerate for up to 3 days.

Sicilian Yellow Pesto
alla Trapanese

MAKES 2½ CUPS

½ cup slivered almonds
3 garlic cloves, sliced
1 teaspoon fine sea salt
¼ teaspoon freshly ground
   black pepper
1 pint yellow or orange
   cherry tomatoes

¾ cup tightly packed fresh basil
   leaves, plus 2 tablespoons
   finely chopped
½ cup extra-virgin olive oil
¾ cup freshly grated
   Parmesan cheese

Toast the almonds in a small skillet over medium heat, about 1 minute.

Combine the almonds, garlic, salt, and pepper in a food processor and pulse until finely ground. Add the tomatoes and ¾ cup of basil leaves and process until smooth.

With the machine running, stream in the olive oil until well combined.

Transfer to a bowl, stir in the cheese and remaining 2 tablespoons chopped basil, and serve.

Transfer to an airtight container and refrigerate for up to 3 days.

Easy Homemade Tahini Sauce

MAKES ¾ CUP

1 cup hulled sesame seeds
2 to 4 tablespoons extra-
   virgin olive oil

1 teaspoon freshly squeezed
   lemon juice (optional)
¼ teaspoon fine sea salt

In a saucepan over medium heat, cook the sesame seeds, stirring constantly, for 4 to 5 minutes, or until they are toasted to a light golden color.

While they are still warm, transfer the sesame seeds to a food processor and process for 1 minute. (Alternatively, you can also grind them in a coffee grinder then add them to the food processor.)

Pour 2 tablespoons of oil into the food processor and process until you have a pourable sauce. You may have to pause and scrape down the sides and process again. Add more oil, if needed to reach the right consistency. Add the lemon juice if using and salt and process again to combine.

Transfer to a clean glass jar with a screw top, seal, and refrigerate. It might taste a bit bitter, but the flavor will become more subtle after it rests in the refrigerator.

Tahini will last for 1 month in the refrigerator.

VARIATION: Add a bit of sugar and vanilla extract and mix for a halvah sauce to drizzle over fruit or yogurt; or add a bit of honey or molasses for a sweeter sauce.

Warm Sauces

MY GRANDMOTHER used to say that warm sauces are for cold days. I agree, yet I won't pass up dipping French fries into my recipe for Steakhouse Blue Cheese and Brandy Sauce (page 192) on a hot summer night. It is a treat I savor slowly and thoroughly enjoy.

Try any of these sauces, any time of the year. I am including my favorite sauces, the ones I cook at home that I love. I always make my Mango Mustard Sauce (page 198) around the holidays and serve it with ham. The Black Cherry Sauce (page 197) is the one I always make when I serve duck, the Classic Blender Hollandaise Sauce with Tarragon (page 194) when I make eggs Benedict.

Steakhouse Blue Cheese and Brandy Sauce

MAKES 2 CUPS

12 ounces blue cheese
1 large garlic clove, minced
1 teaspoon Dijon mustard
½ cup beef broth from a
   beef stock cube

1 cup heavy cream
4 tablespoons brandy
¼ teaspoon freshly ground
   black pepper

Combine all the ingredients in a saucepan over medium-low heat and gently cook for about 6 minutes, stirring constantly, until the sauce is melted and thick.

The sauce can be stored in an airtight container and refrigerated for up to 2 days.

No-Cook Romesco Sauce

MAKES 2 CUPS

3 ounces unsalted slivered
   almonds or hazelnuts
1 slice day-old bread, cut
   into quarters
1 (10- or 12-ounce) jar roasted
   red peppers, drained
1 small red Fresno chile, seeded, sliced
   or ⅛ teaspoon red pepper flakes
1 teaspoon smoked paprika

3 tablespoons tomato paste
2 large garlic cloves
¼ teaspoon fine sea salt
2 tablespoons red wine vinegar
   or sherry vinegar
2 tablespoons fino sherry (optional)
6 tablespoons extra-virgin olive oil
¼ cup tightly packed fresh
   Italian flat-leaf parsley

Combine all the ingredients in a food processor and process until smooth. You can heat up the sauce and serve warm or serve at room temperature.

The sauce can be stored in an airtight container and refrigerated for up to 4 days.

Puttanesca Sauce

MAKES 3½ CUPS

1 recipe for Basic Marinara
 Sauce (recipe follows)
¼ cup capers, drained
¼ cup cured pitted olives or
 kalamatas, finely chopped

¼ teaspoon crushed red
 pepper flakes
Freshly ground black pepper

Combine all the ingredients in a saucepan
over medium-high heat and cook for
about 5 minutes, or until heated through.

Transfer to an airtight container and
refrigerate for up to 4 days or in the
freezer for up to 3 months.

Basic Marinara Sauce

MAKES 3½ CUPS

3 tablespoons extra-virgin olive oil
5 garlic cloves, pressed
1 can anchovies, finely chopped,
 with their oil (optional)
1 teaspoon dried oregano
 or fresh leaves

1 (28-ounce) can whole San Marzano
 Italian tomatoes, drained
1 cup dry red wine or white wine
2 teaspoons granulated sugar
2 tablespoons minced
 fresh basil leaves

Heat the oil in a saucepan over medium heat. Add the garlic and cook for
2 minutes. Add the anchovies and their oil, oregano, tomatoes, and sugar.
Use a potato masher or fork and knife to break up the tomatoes. Bring the
mixture to a boil. Reduce the heat to maintain a simmer and cook, stirring
frequently, for 15 minutes. Stir in the fresh basil leaves and serve.

Transfer to an airtight container and refrigerate for up to 4 days or in the
freezer for up to 3 months.

Italian Clam Sauce for Pasta

MAKES 2½ CUPS

4 tablespoons extra-virgin olive oil
5 garlic cloves, minced
2 shallots, minced
2 oil-packed anchovy fillets,
   finely chopped
¼ teaspoon crushed red
   pepper flakes

⅛ teaspoon dried oregano
1 cup dry white wine
1 (6.5-ounce) can chopped
   clams, with their juice
1 (6.5-ounce) can minced
   clams, with their juice
1½ pounds fresh littleneck clams

Heat the oil in a large saucepan or Dutch oven over medium heat. Add the garlic, shallots, anchovies, red pepper flakes, and oregano and cook for 3 minutes. Add the wine, chopped clams, and minced clams and cook for 1 minute. Add the littleneck clams, cover the pan, and cook for 4 to 5 minutes, or until the clams open. Discard any clams that do not open as they are not good to eat.

To serve, ladle the sauce into individual bowls of pasta and add the clams in their shells on top.

Classic Blender Hollandaise Sauce with Tarragon

MAKES 1 CUP

10 tablespoons unsalted butter
8 fresh tarragon leaves
¼ teaspoon fine sea salt,
   plus more as needed

2 teaspoons freshly squeezed lemon
   juice, plus more as needed
1 teaspoon tarragon vinegar
   or white wine vinegar
3 large egg yolks, room temperature

Melt the butter in a small saucepan and keep it hot over low heat.

Combine the tarragon, salt, lemon juice, vinegar, and egg yolks in a blender and blend for 35 seconds.

With the blender running, very slowly drip the hot butter, drop by drop, into the blender until the mixture is thick. Taste and add more salt or lemon juice, if desired. Blend again and serve immediately.

Coconut Curry Sauce

MAKES 2 CUPS

¼ cup unsalted butter
¼ cup minced onion
2 garlic cloves, pressed
¼ teaspoon crushed red
  pepper flakes
1 tablespoon curry powder
1 chicken stock cube, crumbled

2 tablespoons all-purpose flour
2 cups coconut milk
1 tablespoon soy sauce
2 teaspoons light brown sugar
1 (1-inch) knob fresh ginger,
  peeled and minced
6 leaves fresh basil, thinly sliced

Melt the butter in a saucepan over medium heat. Add the onion and garlic and cook for about 3 minutes, or until almost soft. Add the red pepper flakes, curry powder, crumbled chicken stock cube, and flour and cook, stirring, for 4 minutes. Slowly pour in the coconut milk, soy sauce, brown sugar, and ginger and whisk until combined. Cook, whisking frequently, for 8 minutes, or until the sauce is smooth and thickened. Transfer to a bowl and top with the sliced basil leaves.

The sauce can be stored in an airtight container and refrigerated for up to 4 days.

General Tso's Sauce

MAKES 2 ¼ CUPS

3 tablespoons neutral oil
1 small whole red chiles (or 2 tea-
    spoons crushed red pepper flakes)
6 garlic cloves, thinly sliced
½ cup chicken broth from
    a chicken stock cube
½ cup granulated sugar
½ cup packed light brown sugar
½ cup soy sauce or tamari

2 tablespoons sesame oil
2 tablespoons rice vinegar
¼ cup hoisin sauce
2 teaspoons Chinese five-
    spice powder
1 (2-inch) knob fresh ginger,
    peeled and minced or grated
4 teaspoons cornstarch
¼ cup water

Heat the oil in a wok or large skillet over medium-high heat. Add the chiles and garlic and cook, stirring constantly, for 2 to 3 minutes, or until the garlic is golden brown. Add the chicken broth, sugar, brown sugar, soy sauce, sesame oil, rice vinegar, hoisin sauce, five-spice powder, and ginger and bring to a boil, stirring frequently. Cook for 3 minutes.

In a small bowl, combine the cornstarch and ¼ cup water and mix well. Add the mixture to the sauce and whisk until the sauce thickens. Serve hot.

The sauce can be stored in an airtight container and refrigerated for up to 4 days.

Chinese Restaurant Sweet-and-Sour Sauce

MAKES 2 ½ CUPS

1 cup canned pineapple juice
6 tablespoons rice vinegar
½ cup ketchup
1 ½ tablespoons soy sauce or tamari
⅔ cup granulated sugar

½ teaspoon fine sea salt
1 teaspoon ground ginger
⅛ teaspoon ground cloves
2 tablespoons cornstarch
4 tablespoons water

Combine all the ingredients, except the cornstarch and water, int a saucepan and bring to a boil, stirring frequently, over medium heat. Reduce the heat to maintain a simmer and whisk until the sugar has melted.

In a small bowl, combine the cornstarch and water and mix well. Add the mixture to the sauce and cook, whisking constantly, until the sauce thickens. Taste and add more of any ingredient to your taste.

The sauce can be stored in an airtight container and refrigerated.

Black Cherry Sauce

MAKES 3 CUPS

3 tablespoons extra-virgin
    olive oil or butter
2 medium shallots, minced
2 cups dry red wine, plus
    more as needed
½ cup cherry jam or preserves
¼ teaspoon ground cinnamon

2 tablespoons granulated sugar
Zest and juice of 1 medium
    organic orange
4 tablespoons all-purpose flour
12 ounces frozen, canned, or
    bottled sour dark cherries

Heat the oil in a skillet over medium heat. Add the shallots and cook for 3 minutes. Add the wine, jam, cinnamon, sugar, orange zest, and orange juice and bring to a simmer.

In a small bowl, combine ½ cup of the sauce and the flour and mix well. Pour the mixture back into the saucepan and vigorously whisk while it comes back to a simmer. Cook, stirring frequently, for 5 to 7 minutes, or until the sauce has thickened, adding a bit more wine or water if it's too thick. Add the cherries and cook until they are warmed through. Pour into a serving bowl.

Transfer to an airtight container and refrigerate for up to 1 week.

Warm Blue Cheese Sauce

MAKES 1½ CUPS

1½ cups half-and-half
 or heavy cream
4 ounces blue cheese

Freshly ground black
 pepper, to taste
1 garlic clove, minced
Fine sea salt, as needed

Bring the half-and-half just barely to a boil in a saucepan over medium heat. Take the pan off the heat and whisk in the cheese until it is melted and smooth. Season with pepper and garlic. Taste and add salt if desired. Pour into a serving bowl and serve warm.

Transfer to an airtight container and refrigerate for up to 1 week.

Mango Mustard Sauce

MAKES 4 CUPS

1 mango, pitted, sliced
1 pint light cream
4 tablespoons dry mustard
1 teaspoon Dijon mustard
1 cup packed light brown sugar
1 cup distilled white vinegar

¼ teaspoon fine sea salt
2 egg yolks, well beaten
2 tablespoons all-purpose flour
⅛ teaspoon ground cinnamon
1 to 2 tablespoons Port wine
 or sherry (optional)

Purée the mango slices in a food processor. Combine all the ingredients, except the mango purée and wine, in a double boiler and let simmer over medium heat, whisking frequently, for 30 minutes. Take the pan off the heat and whisk in the mango purée and wine. Serve warm or transfer to an airtight container and refrigerate for up to 3 days.

Basic White Sauce (Béchamel)

MAKES 1¼ CUPS

2 tablespoons unsalted butter
2 tablespoons all-purpose
  flour or Wondra
1¼ cups milk, room temperature

¼ fine sea salt
⅛ teaspoon ground white
  pepper (optional)
⅛ teaspoon ground nutmeg

Melt the butter in a saucepan over medium heat. Add the flour and cook, whisking constantly, for 2 minutes. While whisking constantly, very slowly add the milk and keep whisking until the sauce starts to bubble and has thickened. Whisk in salt, pepper, if using, and nutmeg.

Transfer to an airtight container and refrigerate for up to 4 days.

Mornay Cheese Sauce

MAKES 1¼ CUPS

2 tablespoons unsalted butter
2 tablespoons all-purpose flour
1¼ cups milk, room temperature,
  or chicken or vegetable stock
⅛ teaspoon grated nutmeg
1 teaspoon Dijon mustard

¼ teaspoon sweet paprika
¼ teaspoon fine sea salt
3 tablespoons grated Gruyère
  cheese or your cheese of choice
2 tablespoons grated Parmesan

Melt the butter in a saucepan over medium-low heat. Add the flour and whisk for 2 minutes. Whisking constantly, slowly pour in the milk until well blended. Increase the heat to medium and whisk for 5 to 7 minutes, or until the sauce is smooth and thick. Stir in the remaining ingredients and cook, stirring frequently, until the cheeses are melted. Taste for seasoning.

Transfer to an airtight container and refrigerate for up to 4 days.

Hot Honey and More

HOT HONEY is the new hot condiment. Even big food companies are jumping on the trend and restaurants are increasingly including it on their menus. You won't believe how easy it is to make at home. Here is the basic recipe plus others I make with honey and keep on hand in my refrigerator.

My Favorite Tart Lemon Honey (page 204) recipe doesn't last very long because I use it for everything from smearing it on my toast in the morning to adding it to my tea in the afternoon to offering it with cheeses on a board to using it to coat a chicken before salting it and roasting it.

Easy Homemade Hot Honey

MAKES 1 CUP

1 fresh red Fresno chile
1 cup honey

⅛ teaspoon fine sea salt,
    plus more as needed
Cayenne pepper, as needed

Using rubber or disposable gloves, cut the pepper into strips, keep the seeds, and transfer the pepper and seeds to a medium saucepan.

Grease a measuring cup with oil to make it easier to dispense the honey. Pour the honey into the measuring cup and then pour the honey into the saucepan with the peppers. Add the salt and cook, stirring frequently, over medium-high heat. Press down on the peppers to release their juice and seeds into the honey. When the mixture just barely comes to a simmer, immediately take the pan off the heat and allow to infuse for 30 minutes.

Taste and if it's too "hot" for you, drizzle in more honey until it reaches your desired level of heat. If you want more heat, add a dash of cayenne pepper. Add more salt if you wish.

Pour the hot honey into a clean glass jar with a screw top or a squeeze bottle and enjoy. You can strain out the chiles, but I keep them in my honey.

The hot honey can be stored in the refrigerator for up to 4 days.

Very Cinnamon Honey

MAKES 1 CUP

1 cup honey
2 cinnamon sticks
4 tablespoons ground cinnamon

Combine the honey, cinnamon sticks, and ground cinnamon in a saucepan and cook, stirring frequently, over medium heat for 5 minutes, without allowing it to boil. The kitchen will smell lovely while this cooks!

Take the pan off the heat and allow to cool for 12 to 15 minutes.

Transfer the honey and cinnamon sticks to a clean glass jar with a screw top, seal, and store in the refrigerator. The ground cinnamon will eventually float to the top.

Honey with Walnuts

MAKES 3 CUPS

1 cup raw unsalted walnut halves
2 cups honey
1 tablespoon light brown sugar

1 teaspoon vanilla extract
¼ teaspoon fine sea salt

Preheat the oven to 325 degrees F.

Spread out the nuts on a baking sheet and bake for 2 to 5 minutes, or until they are to toasted a light brown and you can smell their fragrance. Allow the walnuts to cool to room temperature.

Divide the nuts between 2 clean glass jars with screw tops. Set aside.

Grease a measuring cup with oil to make it easier to dispense the honey. Pour the honey into the measuring cup and then pour the honey into a saucepan over medium heat.

Add the sugar, vanilla, and salt and whisk just until the sugar is dissolved. Divide the honey equally into the jars to cover the nuts. Let the honey cool to room temperature so it solidifies a bit, and then push down the nuts and seal with the tops.

My Favorite Tart Lemon Honey

MAKES 1 CUP

1 cup honey

2 large organic lemons

Grease a measuring cup with oil to make it easier to dispense the honey. Pour the honey into the measuring cup and then pour the honey into a saucepan. Grate both lemons on the large holes of a box grater. Add the grated peel to the saucepan with the honey. Cut 4 thin slices from 1 lemon, cut each slice into quarters, and add them to the saucepan. (Add more lemon slices if you wish.)

Cook over medium heat for 6 minutes, without allowing it to boil. Take the pan off the heat and let sit for 5 minutes.

Transfer to a clean glass jar with a screw top, seal, and store in the refrigerator for up to 1 month.

The honey can be stored in the refrigerator for up to 2 months. Bring to room temperature to serve.

Hot Honey Fruit Mostarda

MAKES 2 CUPS

1 fresh red Fresno chile
1 cup honey
1 shallot, finely chopped
⅛ teaspoon fine sea salt
1 teaspoon yellow mustard seeds

¼ to ½ cup distilled white vinegar
   or white wine vinegar
2 teaspoons Dijon mustard
1 cup dried apricots, finely chopped
½ cup dried cherries, finely chopped

Using rubber or disposable gloves, cut the pepper into strips, keep the seeds, and transfer the pepper and seeds to a medium saucepan.

Grease a measuring cup with oil to make it easier to dispense the honey. Pour the honey into the measuring cup and then pour the honey into a saucepan.

Add the shallot, salt, mustard seeds, vinegar, and mustard and cook, stirring frequently, over medium heat until it barely comes to a simmer. Take the pan off the heat, add the apricots and cherries, and stir well. Return the pan to the stove and bring the mixture back to a simmer over medium heat. Cook for about 10 minutes, or until the fruit are plump and the mixture begins to thicken. Allow to cool to room temperature.

Transfer the mixture to 1 or 2 clean glass jars with screw tops, seal, and refrigerate for up to 1 month.

Light and Fluffy Whipped Honey

MAKES AS MUCH AS DESIRED

Plain liquid honey, crystallized honey, or hot honey in desired amount

Instant coffee, maple syrup, vanilla extract, or ground cinnamon (optional)

Add the honey and the flavoring of choice to taste, if using, to a stand mixer with the whisk attachment and beat on medium speed to whip air into it for 20 to 30 minutes, until it changes color and looks pale and fluffy.

Transfer the whipped honey to clean glass jar(s) with screw tops and store in a cool place if not using right away. After a week or so it may separate but it is still usable, and you can always whip it again if you want.

Dessert Sauces

TRY PRESENTING SEVERAL sweet dessert sauces to go with ice cream or cake or pie on a long board along with serving spoons and watch everyone's eyes light up! This is one of the most popular endings to a meal that I make: a condiment board with a row of toppings and sauces for people to help themselves, like a buffet of treats to drizzle, dollop, and sprinkle.

You can take any of the dessert sauce recipes below and put interesting twists on them. Use limes or blood oranges or grapefruit instead or oranges in the Orange Custard Sauce (page 210). Whisk some Irish cream liqueur into the Warm Butter Pecan Sauce (page 210). Melt some peanut butter into the Warm Chocolate Sauce (page 208). Or crush candy canes into small pieces and swirl them into the Easy Eggnog Dessert Sauce (page 214) for the holidays. Anything goes.

Warm Chocolate Sauce

MAKES 1¼ CUP

¾ cup heavy cream
1 teaspoon vanilla extract
2 tablespoons unsalted butter
1 tablespoon instant
    espresso powder

1 teaspoon ground cinnamon
⅛ teaspoon fine sea salt
1 cup semisweet chocolate chips

In a small saucepan over medium-low heat, combine the cream, vanilla, butter, espresso powder, cinnamon, and salt and cook, stirring frequently, until the butter is melted. Add half of the chocolate chips and stir until melted. Add the remaining chocolate chips and stir until you reach the consistency you desire. Serve hot.

The sauce can be stored in an airtight container and refrigerated for up to 1 month.

Chocolate Caramel Sauce

MAKES 2 CUPS

½ cup water
½ teaspoon fine sea salt
1 cup granulated sugar
1 cup heavy whipping cream, room
    temperature or slightly warmed
1 ½ teaspoons vanilla extract
8 ounces semisweet chocolate chips
2 tablespoons butter

Combine the water, salt, and sugar
in a saucepan over medium-high heat
and bring to a boil, stirring constantly to

dissolve the sugar. Reduce the heat to medium and cook for 5 to 10 minutes, without stirring, until it turns a golden amber color.

Take the pan off the heat. Slowly pour the cream into the caramel, being careful as it might splatter, and quickly whisk to combine. Add the vanilla and chocolate chips and stir until melted. Add the butter and stir until it is melted. Serve warm.

The sauce can be stored in an airtight container and refrigerated for up to 2 weeks. Heat up the sauce before serving.

Sea Salt Caramel Sauce

MAKES 1½ CUPS

½ cup heavy cream, room
   temperature
2 tablespoons unsalted butter,
   room temperature
½ teaspoon fine sea salt

1 teaspoon vanilla extract
1 cup granulated sugar
¼ cup water
½ teaspoon coarse sea
   salt flakes (optional)

Combine the cream, butter, fine sea salt, and vanilla in a saucepan over medium-low heat and gently warm the mixture, stirring frequently, until the butter is melted. Keep warm.

Combine the sugar and water in a nonstick skillet over medium heat and cook, stirring frequently, for about 10 minutes, or until the sugar has melted and the mixture has turned a caramel color. Take the skillet off the heat.

Slowly pour the warm cream mixture into the caramel, being careful as it might splatter, and quickly whisk to combine. Keep warm on the stove or in the oven until ready to use. Garnish with coarse sea salt flakes, if desired.

The sauce can be stored in an airtight container and refrigerated for up to 2 weeks. Heat up the caramel before serving.

Warm Butter Pecan Sauce

MAKES 2½ CUPS

2 cups pecan halves
2 sticks unsalted butter
¾ cup packed light brown
　　sugar or maple syrup

¼ teaspoon fine sea salt
2 teaspoons vanilla extract
¼ cup evaporated milk or
　　heavy whipping cream

Spread out the pecan halves in a large skillet over medium heat and toast them for about 5 minutes, or until you can smell their aroma. Transfer the pecans to a plate and reserve.

Combine the rest of the ingredients in a saucepan over medium-low heat and cook for about 2 minutes, stirring frequently, until the sugar is melted. Fold in the pecans and serve the sauce warm.

The sauce can be stored in an airtight container and refrigerated for up to 2 weeks.

Orange Custard Sauce

MAKES 3 CUPS

2 cups milk
¼ cup heavy cream
Zest and juice of 1 organic orange
4 teaspoons pure orange extract
¼ teaspoon vanilla extract

2 teaspoons all-purpose flour
2 tablespoons water
8 large egg yolks, room temperature
½ cup granulated sugar

In a large saucepan, combine the milk, cream, orange juice, orange extract, and vanilla and bring just to a boil over medium-high heat. Reduce the heat but keep the mixture hot.

In a cup, mix together the flour with water. Pour the mixture into the pan and whisk to combine. Bring the mixture back to a boil and remove from the heat.

In a stand mixer or using a hand mixer and bowl, beat the egg yolks for 1 minute. Add the sugar and beat for 1 minute, or until the eggs are pale yellow and thick.

Vigorously whisk ½ cup of the hot milk mixture into the egg mixture. Pour the egg mixture into the saucepan and whisk over low heat until the custard thickens enough to coat the back of a spoon. Do not let the mixture boil.

Remove the pan from the heat and whisk in the orange zest. Allow the mixture to cool to room temperature.

Transfer the custard to a container, cover with plastic wrap that touches the custard to prevent a skin forming, and refrigerate until ready to use. Thin out the custard with a little orange juice, if needed, before serving.

The custard can be refrigerated for up to 4 days.

Fluffy Yogurt-Lemon Sauce

MAKES 2 CUPS

1 cup Greek yogurt
Zest and 1 tablespoon juice
    of 1 organic lemon

½ teaspoon vanilla extract
½ cup heavy whipping cream
4 tablespoons confectioners' sugar

Combine the yogurt, lemon zest, and lemon juice in a bowl and whisk to combine. Reserve.

In another bowl, whip the cream with an electric hand mixer until soft peaks form. Add the sugar and continue beating until stiff peaks form.

Fold the reserved yogurt mixture into the whipped cream until combined. Cover and refrigerate before using.

The sauce can be stored in an airtight container and refrigerated for up to 4 days.

Grand Marnier Orange Sauce

MAKES 1¼ CUPS

Juice of 3 organic oranges (⅔ cup juice), plus 1 orange zested
⅔ cups granulated sugar or confectioners' sugar
⅛ teaspoon fine sea salt
5 tablespoons salted butter, room temperature
3 tablespoons Grand Marnier

Combine the orange juice, orange zest, sugar, and salt in a saucepan over medium heat and whisk until the sugar is melted.

Add the butter and whisk until melted and the sauce is glossy. Add the Grand Marnier and cook, stirring frequently, for 4 minutes. Serve warm.

The sauce can be stored in an airtight container and refrigerated for up to 1 week. Heat up the sauce before serving.

Limoncello Lemon Curd Sauce

MAKES 2 CUPS

½ cup heavy cream
1 cup granulated sugar
1 egg yolk
¼ cup freshly squeezed lemon juice
¼ cup limoncello
½ cup (1 stick) unsalted butter

Combine the cream and sugar in a heavy saucepan or Dutch oven over medium heat. Cook, whisking constantly, until the sugar has melted. Take the pan off the heat.

Add the egg yolk and vigorously whisk until thoroughly combined. Pour in the lemon juice and Limoncello, add the butter, and return the pan to the stove. Cook, whisking constantly, over medium-low heat until the butter has melted and you can see little bubbles around the edges and a bit of steam rising (you may have to raise the temperature a bit). Allow to cool to room temperature.

The sauce can be stored in an airtight container and refrigerated for up to 4 days.

Dark Chocolate Balsamic Drizzle

MAKES 2 CUPS

2 cups dark balsamic vinegar
½ cup granulated sugar
¼ teaspoon fine sea salt
1 cup water
½ teaspoon ground cinnamon

⅛ teaspoon ground nutmeg
1 teaspoon vanilla extract
⅔ cup dark Dutch process
   cocoa powder
Pinch cayenne (optional)

Cook the balsamic vinegar in a saucepan over medium-low heat and reduce it, stirring frequently, for 20 to 25 minutes, or until there is only 1 cup left and it is thick and coats the back of a spoon. Take the pan off the heat and reserve.

Combine the sugar, salt, and water in another saucepan and bring to a boil over medium heat, whisking constantly until the sugar melts. Add the rest of the ingredients including the cayenne, if using, and cook, whisking frequently, for 5 to 7 minutes, or until it thickens. Take the pan off the heat and allow to cool to room temperature.

Transfer the mixture into the reserved balsamic syrup and whisk to combine. Serve in a small pitcher or bowl.

The sauce can be stored in an airtight container and refrigerated.

Easy Eggnog Dessert Sauce

MAKES 1½ CUPS

1 (14-ounce) can sweetened
   condensed milk
¼ cup water or milk
¼ teaspoon salt
2 teaspoons vanilla bean
   paste or vanilla extract

⅛ teaspoon ground nutmeg
⅛ teaspoon ground cinnamon
1 or 2 tablespoons rum, whiskey,
   or brandy (optional)

Combine the condensed milk, water, and salt in a saucepan over medium heat and cook, stirring constantly, for 2 minutes. Take the pan off the heat and whisk in the vanilla, nutmeg, cinnamon, and rum, if using. Serve warm or cold.

The sauce can be stored in an airtight container and refrigerated for up to 4 days.

Strawberry and White Chocolate Sauce

MAKES 1½ CUPS

16 ounces fresh strawberries,
   hulled and quartered
¼ cup plus 1 tablespoon granulated sugar, divided
1 (4-ounce) high-quality white chocolate
   bar, broken into chunks
1 teaspoon vanilla extract

Combine the strawberries and ¼ cup of sugar in a saucepan over medium heat and bring to a boil, stirring constantly until the sugar melts. Reduce the heat to medium and cook, stirring frequently, for about 1 minute. Use a potato masher or fork to mash the berries down and continue to cook for 1 to 2 more minutes, or until the strawberries soften.

Take the pan off the heat, transfer the mixture to a blender or food processor while it's still hot, and process until very smooth.

Add the chocolate and vanilla and process until velvety smooth. Taste and add the remaining 1 tablespoon of sugar, if needed. It will depend upon how ripe your strawberries were. Serve warm or cold.

The sauce can be stored in an airtight container and refrigerated for up to 4 days.

Homemade Sweet Mascarpone

MAKES 2 CUPS

2 cups heavy whipping cream
1 ½ teaspoons freshly
squeezed lemon juice

1 teaspoon vanilla extract (optional)
2 tablespoons confectioners'
sugar (optional)

Heat the heavy cream in a medium saucepan over low heat, and gently bring to 180 to 185 degrees F on a thermometer. Stir frequently to help the water evaporate from the cream as it heats.

Take the pan off the heat. Stir in the fresh lemon juice and stir for a few minutes until you see the cream starting to get thick. Cover and let sit at room temperature for 1 hour.

Place a clean dishcloth or double layer of cheesecloth inside a fine-mesh strainer set over a bowl. Pour the cream into the dishcloth or cheesecloth so that the liquid can drain down into the bowl below. Cover with plastic wrap and refrigerate for 24 hours.

Transfer the mascarpone to a bowl and discard the liquid. You can use the mascarpone as is or add the vanilla and confectioners' sugar to sweeten it.

The mascarpone can be stored in an airtight container and refrigerated for up to 4 days.

Cannoli Dip for Fruit

MAKES 3 CUPS

2 cups whole-milk ricotta
  cheese, drained through
  cheesecloth until dry
8 ounces mascarpone cheese
  or cream cheese, softened
1 cup confectioners' sugar

2 teaspoons vanilla extract
¼ to ½ teaspoon ground cinnamon
⅛ teaspoon fine sea salt
1 cup mini chocolate chips or
  high-quality chocolate grated
  on a hand grater (optional)

Combine the ricotta, mascarpone, sugar, vanilla, cinnamon, and salt in a stand mixer or in a bowl with a handheld electric mixer and beat until very smooth. Taste and adjust the seasoning. Stir in the chocolate chips or grated chocolate, if using, and serve.

The sauce can be stored in an airtight container and refrigerated for up to 1 week.

Raspberry Chambord Sauce

MAKES ABOUT 2¼ CUPS

1 (10-ounce) package frozen
  raspberries, thawed
½ cup granulated sugar or
  confectioners' sugar
7 tablespoons water, plus
  more as needed

1 tablespoon fresh lemon juice
1 teaspoon vanilla extract
2 tablespoons Chambord raspberry
  liqueur, plus more as needed

Combine all the ingredients in a blender and process until smooth. Add more Chambord or water, if desired. The sauce can be stored in an airtight container and refrigerated for up to 1 week.

Cheesecake Sauce

MAKES 1¼ CUPS

1 (8-ounce) package cream cheese
2 teaspoons vanilla extract
3 teaspoons fresh lemon juice

3 to 4 tablespoons confectioners'
sugar, plus more as needed
2 tablespoons sour cream
1 tablespoon whole milk (optional)

Combine all the ingredients in a food processor and process until very smooth. Taste and add more sugar if desired and thin out with milk, if needed. Serve in a bowl for dipping.

The sauce can be stored in an airtight container and refrigerated for up to 1 week.

Homemade
Marshmallow Cream

MAKES 1 CUP

2 cups mini marshmallows
1 tablespoon corn syrup, maple syrup, or honey
1 tablespoon water

If you are using a double boiler, spray the top section where you will melt the marshmallows with cooking spray. If you are using a heatproof bowl set over a pot of simmering water as your double boiler, spray the inside of the bowl.

Spray a rubber spatula with cooking spray. Gently melt the marshmallows in the double boiler, using the rubber spatula to mix. When they are halfway melted, add the corn syrup and water and stir with the spatula until the mixture is very smooth. Transfer to a bowl to serve.

The marshmallow cream can be stored in an airtight container and refrigerated.

Acknowledgments

As always, I want to express deep gratitude to my longtime agent and friend, Deborah Ritchken.

To my loyal recipe testers, I thank you from the bottom of my heart, especially Barbara Michelson, Sarah Hodge, and Mike Morin.

To Michelle Branson, my wonderful editor at Gibbs Smith, you make the experience of creating something beautiful a reality for me and I am forever grateful for your wisdom and kindness.

As always, my sincere thanks go to the entire team at Gibbs Smith for their extreme professionalism, enthusiasm, and for designing such beautiful books.

Index

Spreads

Sugars

Vinegars

Metric Conversion Chart

Volume Measurements		Weight Measurements		Temperature	
U.S.	Metric	U.S.	Metric	Fahrenheit	Celsius
1 teaspoon	5 ml	½ ounce	15 g	250	120
1 tablespoon	15 ml	1 ounce	30 g	300	150
¼ cup	60 ml	3 ounces	80 g	325	160
⅓ cup	80 ml	4 ounces	115 g	350	175
½ cup	125 ml	8 ounces	225 g	375	190
⅔ cup	160 ml	12 ounces	340 g	400	200
¾ cup	180 ml	1 pound	450 g	425	220
1 cup	250 ml	2¼ pounds	1 kg	450	230

About the Author

Hillary Davis is a cookbook author, contributing journalist, cooking instructor, and lecturer. After the critical success of her first book, *A Million A Minute*, a book agent who knew about Hillary's love of all things food approached her and convinced her to write a cookbook.

Hillary wrote her first cookbook, *Cuisine Niçoise* while living in the south of France in the hilltop village of Bar-sur-Loup on the French Riviera. *Cuisine Niçoise* celebrated the healthy style of cooking prepared in the countryside around her home near Nice.

In *French Comfort Food* she went on a delicious journey throughout the many regions of France to re-discover the most loved meals that French families prepare every day at home. She has written three more French cookbooks: *Le French Oven*, *French Desserts*, and *French From the Market*, as well as a cookbook about the cooking and farm markets in the Hamptons, called *The Hamptons Kitchen*. Hillary also writes a popular weekly Substack newsletter called *DestinationFood*.

Hillary has a degree in economics from Columbia University in New York and a graduate degree in international relations from Cambridge University in England. She currently lives in the Hamptons, New York City, and lives several months a year in France.